STAR WARS
THE HIGH REPUBLIC

CHARACTER
ENCYCLOPEDIA

WRITTEN BY MEGAN CROUSE AND AMY RICHAU
COVER ART BY PHIL NOTO

CONTENTS

FOREWORD

It is impossible to speak of *The High Republic* without mentioning the people who created it. The people who found themselves in the characters. The people of our little part of the internet who made friends and found comfort and hope through our mutual love of *The High Republic*. Would we ever have thought that this corner of the galaxy, which years ago we couldn't have even comprehended, would bring us all together in one of our darkest times?

2020 was a hard year for all of us. A year of tremendous loss, isolation, and more fear than hope. Personally, I was a new mom with postpartum depression and a loss that had shaken my world. I didn't see much to look forward to. Then I received a message that changed my life. Would I like to host a bi-monthly show on StarWars.com that covered the still codenamed "Project Luminous"? I said, "YES!"

Little did I know what would come from that "Yes." I didn't know that it would bring me "The Luminous Five," Cavan Scott, Charles Soule, Claudia Gray, Justina Ireland, and Daniel José Older. Alongside Lucasfilm Editorial and Story Group, the Five are the architects of Phase I of *The High Republic*. People who not only touched me with their words but with their acts of kindness. I also came into contact with so many wonderful and dedicated teams at Lucasfilm, especially the Online team and everyone involved in *The High Republic Show*. Each person brings their immense talent to every bit of content.

Our *High Republic* family continued to grow with the Phase II additions of Kristin Baver, Lydia Kang, Tessa Gratton, George Mann, and Zoraida Córdova. It continues to grow with Phase III (hi, Alyssa Wong). It grows with the book you hold in your hands now, which welcomes Amy Richau and Megan Crouse to our ever-expanding family.

We all have the piece of *Star Wars* that serves as our entry point into a lifetime of fandom. If this book is your first foray into *The High Republic*, or even *Star Wars*: welcome. May you fall in love with the characters. May you feel welcome into this community that will greet you with love and light. May the pictures and stories spark your curiosity and imagination. May they remind you that no matter how dark the days may seem, we all share a love of story and *Star Wars* that can serve as a light in the dark... a beacon if you will.

Krystina Arielle
Host of *Star Wars: The High Republic Show*

INTRODUCTION

The High Republic era, approximately 500–100 years before the fall of the Republic, is a golden age of progress. The Galactic Republic and Jedi Order work together as explorers and peacekeepers, heading ever further into the deepest reaches of the galaxy to help those in need. Hyperspace prospectors, such as the powerful Graf and San Tekka families, seek their fortunes and expand the frontier by discovering new routes through hyperspace.

It is a time of industry and splendor. The Republic and the Jedi work together to build the space station Starlight Beacon, which stands as a glorious testament to this period of cooperation and prosperity. The Jedi Order builds outposts in far-flung regions where it believes its presence can make a difference.

The galaxy is home to many groups who, like the Jedi, are centered around a connection or devotion to the Force. Some of these sects have more extreme philosophies than others, but the Convocation of the Force—a group based in the Holy City of Jedha—aims to bring them all together, to reach an understanding, and to build relationships.

Much of the galaxy is still undiscovered by the Republic, and dangers from the unknown are hard to foresee. Pirates and mercenaries attack remote communities and travelers. Criminal organizations, such as the Hutts, wield great influence in the areas under their control. And groups such as the mysterious Path of the Open Hand and, later, the chaotic and ruthless Nihil, seek to gain power by attacking the Jedi Order.

HOW TO USE THIS BOOK

Star Wars: The High Republic: Character Encyclopedia
is an exploration of more than 275 characters, offering
information about their backgrounds and fates. Entries
in this book are organized according to the faction with
which each character is associated. There is also an
index at the back of the book.

The dating system in the book uses BBY, an indicator of
how many years before the Battle of Yavin an event
takes place. The Battle of Yavin was a critical event first
depicted in *Star Wars:* Episode IV *A New Hope.*

The High Republic publishing initiative is split into three
phases. There are icons in the top right corners of entries
to signify which phase the characters appear in.

PHASE II
The Quest of the Jedi
c.500 BBY–382 BBY

PHASE I
The Light of the Jedi
252 BBY–229 BBY

PHASE III
The Trials of the Jedi
229 BBY–c.220 BBY

KEY TO FIRST APPEARANCES IN DATA FILES

Each character's data file refers to their first appearance within a piece of High Republic media. For example, the legendary Maz Kanata debuted in *Star Wars: Episode VII The Force Awakens*, but her data file lists her first appearance as *Star Wars: The High Republic Adventures (Phase I)*. Any characters that do not currently feature in any High Republic media will list their first appearance in a piece of *Star Wars* media set during the timeframe of the High Republic.

AToC	*Star Wars: The High Republic – A Test of Courage*	**TfGE**	*Star Wars: Tales from Galaxy's Edge*
Cat	*Star Wars: The High Republic – Cataclysm*	**TfGE: LC**	*Star Wars: Tales from Galaxy's Edge: Last Call*
Con	*Star Wars: The High Republic – Convergence*	**TFS**	*Star Wars: The High Republic – The Fallen Star*
EfV	*Star Wars: The High Republic – Escape from Valo*	**THR (PI)**	*Star Wars: The High Republic (Marvel comic series) 2021*
ItD	*Star Wars: The High Republic – Into the Dark*	**THR (PII)**	*Star Wars: The High Republic (Marvel comic series) 2022*
J: S	*Star Wars Jedi: Survivor*		
LD	*Star Wars: Life Day*	**THR: EotS**	*Star Wars: The High Republic – The Eye of the Storm*
LotJ	*Star Wars: The High Republic – Light of the Jedi*		
MH	*Star Wars: The High Republic – Midnight Horizon*	**THR: TB**	*Star Wars: The High Republic – The Blade*
MtD	*Star Wars: The High Republic – Mission to Disaster*	**THR: ToS**	*Star Wars: The High Republic – Trail of Shadows*
		THRA (PI)	*Star Wars: The High Republic Adventures 2021*
OotS	*Star Wars: The High Republic – Out of the Shadows*	**THRA (PII)**	*Star Wars: The High Republic Adventures 2022*
PoD	*Star Wars: The High Republic – Path of Deceit*	**THRA: A**	*Star Wars: The High Republic Adventures Annual*
PoV	*Star Wars: The High Republic – Path of Vengeance*	**THRA: QotJ**	*Star Wars: The High Republic Adventures – Quest of the Jedi*
QfPX	*Star Wars: The High Republic – Quest for Planet X*		
QftHC	*Star Wars: The High Republic – Quest for the Hidden City*	**THRA: TGBOS**	*Star Wars: The High Republic Adventures – The Galactic Bake-Off Spectacular*
RtCT	*Star Wars: The High Republic – Race to Crashpoint Tower*	**THRA: TMoTP**	*Star Wars: The High Republic Adventures – The Monster of Temple Peak*
SS: FD	*Star Wars: The High Republic – Starlight: First Duty*	**THRA: TNT**	*Star Wars: The High Republic Adventures – The Nameless Terror*
SS: GT	*Star Wars: The High Republic – Starlight: Go Together*	**THRS**	*Star Wars: The High Republic Show*
SS: PM	*Star Wars: The High Republic – Starlight: Past Mistakes*	**ToE: ADP**	*Star Wars: The High Republic – Tales of Enlightenment: A Different Perspective*
SS: SR	*Star Wars: The High Republic – Starlight: Shadows Remain*	**ToE: LO**	*Star Wars: The High Republic – Tales of Enlightenment: Last Orders*
TBoJ	*Star Wars: The High Republic – The Battle of Jedha*	**ToE: NP**	*Star Wars: The High Republic – Tales of Enlightenment: New Prospects*
TEoB, V1	*Star Wars: The High Republic – The Edge of Balance volume 1*	**ToLaL**	*Star Wars: The High Republic – Tales of Light and Life*
TEoB, V2	*Star Wars: The High Republic – The Edge of Balance volume 2*	**TR**	*Star Wars: The High Republic – Tempest Runner*
TEoB: P	*Star Wars: The High Republic – The Edge of Balance: Precedent*	**TRS**	*Star Wars: The High Republic – The Rising Storm*
		YJA	*Star Wars: Young Jedi Adventures*
TEoD	*Star Wars: The High Republic – The Eye of Darkness*	**Yod**	*Star Wars: Yoda*

c.500 BBY–382 BBY

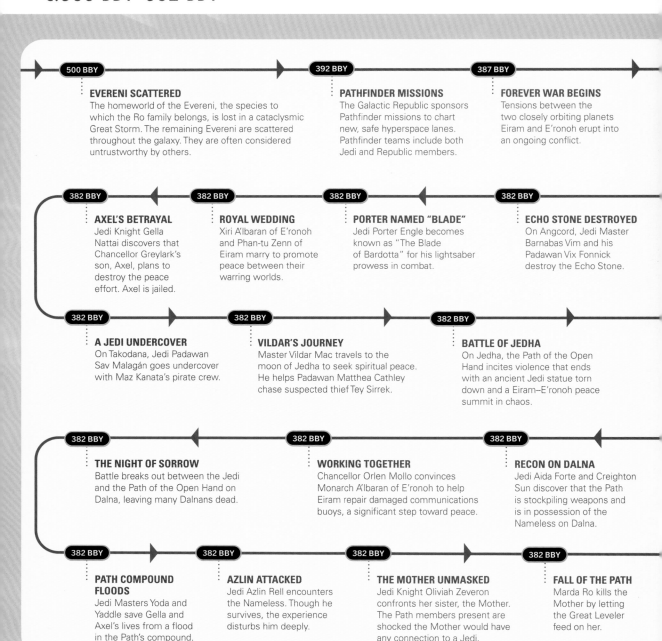

500 BBY

EVERENI SCATTERED
The homeworld of the Evereni, the species to which the Ro family belongs, is lost in a cataclysmic Great Storm. The remaining Evereni are scattered throughout the galaxy. They are often considered untrustworthy by others.

392 BBY

PATHFINDER MISSIONS
The Galactic Republic sponsors Pathfinder missions to chart new, safe hyperspace lanes. Pathfinder teams include both Jedi and Republic members.

387 BBY

FOREVER WAR BEGINS
Tensions between the two closely orbiting planets Eiram and E'ronoh erupt into an ongoing conflict.

382 BBY

AXEL'S BETRAYAL
Jedi Knight Gella Nattai discovers that Chancellor Greylark's son, Axel, plans to destroy the peace effort. Axel is jailed.

382 BBY

ROYAL WEDDING
Xiri A'lbaran of E'ronoh and Phan-tu Zenn of Eiram marry to promote peace between their warring worlds.

382 BBY

PORTER NAMED "BLADE"
Jedi Porter Engle becomes known as "The Blade of Bardotta" for his lightsaber prowess in combat.

382 BBY

ECHO STONE DESTROYED
On Angcord, Jedi Master Barnabas Vim and his Padawan Vix Fonnick destroy the Echo Stone.

382 BBY

A JEDI UNDERCOVER
On Takodana, Jedi Padawan Sav Malagán goes undercover with Maz Kanata's pirate crew.

382 BBY

VILDAR'S JOURNEY
Master Vildar Mac travels to the moon of Jedha to seek spiritual peace. He helps Padawan Matthea Cathley chase suspected thief Tey Sirrek.

382 BBY

BATTLE OF JEDHA
On Jedha, the Path of the Open Hand incites violence that ends with an ancient Jedi statue torn down and a Eiram–E'ronoh peace summit in chaos.

382 BBY

THE NIGHT OF SORROW
Battle breaks out between the Jedi and the Path of the Open Hand on Dalna, leaving many Dalnans dead.

382 BBY

WORKING TOGETHER
Chancellor Orlen Mollo convinces Monarch A'lbaran of E'ronoh to help Eiram repair damaged communications buoys, a significant step toward peace.

382 BBY

RECON ON DALNA
Jedi Aida Forte and Creighton Sun discover that the Path is stockpiling weapons and is in possession of the Nameless on Dalna.

382 BBY

PATH COMPOUND FLOODS
Jedi Masters Yoda and Yaddle save Gella and Axel's lives from a flood in the Path's compound.

382 BBY

AZLIN ATTACKED
Jedi Azlin Rell encounters the Nameless. Though he survives, the experience disturbs him deeply.

382 BBY

THE MOTHER UNMASKED
Jedi Knight Oliviah Zeveron confronts her sister, the Mother. The Path members present are shocked the Mother would have any connection to a Jedi.

382 BBY

FALL OF THE PATH
Marda Ro kills the Mother by letting the Great Leveler feed on her.

Much of the galaxy is unknown, just waiting to be discovered. Republic Pathfinder teams and independent prospectors map out unexplored areas of space. Co-Chancellor Kyong Greylark serves the Republic at its heart on Coruscant, while Co-Chancellor Orlen Mollo reaches out to people in the more distant star systems. On Dalna, the Path of the Open Hand group steals Force-affiliated artifacts. The Path unleashes mysterious creatures, known as the Nameless.

383 BBY

HYPERSPACE RUSH
Independent prospectors compete to map hyperspace lanes for profit. Two rival families, the Grafs and the San Tekkas, are the most influential groups of prospectors.

385 BBY

THE PATH REMADE
The Mother, known as Elecia Zeveron, takes over the group called the Path of the Open Hand.

382 BBY

PROSPECTORS FIND PLANET X
Prospectors Radicaz "Sunshine" Dobbs and Spence and Dass Leffbruk explore the mysterious Planet X. The Leffbruks' ship crashes, and Sunshine rescues them in his own ship only to strand them on Aubadas later.

382 BBY

DEATH ON DALNA
Jedi Zallah Macri and Kevmo Zink are killed by the Nameless under the Mother's command.

382 BBY

SHOWDOWN ON AUBADAS
Jedi Master Silandra Sho's Pathfinder team goes to Aubadas looking for Buran.

382 BBY

FIGHT AGAINST THE NAMELESS
Jedi Master Rok Buran and a Pathfinder team confront the Nameless, taking heavy losses.

382 BBY

CHANGING BASES
The Path of the Open Hand flees to Jedha on board its flagship, the *Gaze Electric*.

382 BBY

INVESTIGATING THE ATTACK
Master Silandra Sho and Jedha local Keth Cerapath investigate the attack on the peace summit.

382 BBY

THE ROD OF SEASONS
Vildar Mac and Tey Sirrek fight Path members Yana Ro and the Herald for weapons that can control the Nameless. Yana is left with the Rod of Seasons, and the Rod of Daybreak is lost.

382 BBY

THE CEASEFIRE BROKEN
A crashed ship on the moon Eirie, planted by the Path, destroys the fragile peace between Eiram and E'ronoh.

382 BBY

NEGOTIATIONS COMMENCE
Yoda sends Master Char-Ryl-Roy and Padawan Enya Keen to Eiram and E'ronoh. They convince Xiri A'lbaran to join them as they confront the Path on Dalna.

382 BBY

AXEL FREED
Jedi Gella Nattai and Orin Darhga release Axel Greylark from prison to learn about the Path's plans.

382 BBY

RETURN TO PLANET X
Path member Marda Ro and Sunshine Dobbs travel to Planet X to harvest Nameless eggs.

382 BBY

MARDA RO IN CHARGE
Marda takes command of the Path, the *Gaze Electric*, and the *Leveler*. She also holds the Rod of Seasons.

382 BBY

HYPERSPACE CHASE
Dass Leffbruk and Padawan Rooper Nitani join the Hyperspace Chase contest as part of their plan to retrieve Dass' lost ship from Planet X.

382 BBY

NEW PEACE TREATY
The rulers of Eiram and E'ronoh celebrate peace between their worlds. A new hyperspace lane is opened to connect the two planets to the Hetzal system.

THE LIGHT OF THE JEDI

252 BBY–229 BBY

252 BBY

THE NIHIL EXPAND
Asgar Ro names himself as Eye of the Nihil. He grows the organization using hyperspace paths acquired from his captive, Mari San Tekka.

242 BBY

A NEW EYE
After Nihil Tempest Runner Lourna Dee fatally stabs Asgar, his son Marchion seizes power, becoming the new Eye of the Nihil.

c.234 BBY

NEW CHANCELLOR
Lina Soh from the planet Daghee is elected Supreme Chancellor of the Galactic Republic.

232 BBY

GREAT DISASTER
The Republic ship *Legacy Run* collides with an obstacle flying through a hyperspace lane. The debris from this accident threatens the Hetzal system until the Jedi arrive.

231 BBY

DEFENSE OF BANCHII
Jedi Knight Lily Tora-Asi helps lead an effort to save the Jedi outpost on Banchii from the Drengir.

231 BBY

FIGHT AGAINST THE DRENGIR
The Jedi learn that the Drengir are controlled by the Great Progenitor on the planet Mulita.

232 BBY

JEDI MYSTERY
Jedi Master Yoda mysteriously disappears after the Battle of Quantxi.

232 BBY

STARLIGHT BEACON
A ceremony marks the official opening of the Outer Rim space station Starlight Beacon, one of Chancellor Soh's Great Works.

231 BBY

REPUBLIC FAIR ATTACK
Soh opens the Republic Fair, another of her Great Works, on Valo. Shortly after, a Nihil fleet arrives and bombs the celebration. During a fierce battle, Lourna Dee attempts to assassinate Soh. The Republic and Jedi mistakenly believe Lourna to be the leader of the Nihil.

231 BBY

VICTORY ON MULITA
The Jedi and the Hutts join forces to take down the Drengir on Mulita.

231 BBY

CYCLOR BETRAYAL
Marchion and Lourna Dee betray Nihil Tempest Leader Pan Eyta in a battle with the Republic at Cyclor.

230 BBY

OCCLUSION ZONE
The Nihil claim 10 galactic sectors. These areas are enclosed by a barrier that prevents hyperspace travel without permission of the Nihil. Republic attempts to breach the barrier are unsuccessful.

230 BBY

NIHIL CELEBRATION
While rescue efforts are ongoing near the crash site on Eiram, the Jedi are recalled to Coruscant. Marchion announces to the galaxy that he is the leader of the Nihil.

230 BBY

FALL OF STARLIGHT
A Nihil assault on Starlight Beacon sees Nameless creatures let loose on the station. In the chaos, they kill several Jedi. Stellan Gios and Estala Maru sacrifice their lives to save others but the station is destroyed, crashing into Eiram's ocean. Senator Ghirra Starros—a Nihil spy—returns to Marchion's side.

229 BBY

SESSION IN THE SENATE
The Jedi Order assembles within the Senate chamber on Coruscant. A set of emergency orders is issued by the Jedi Council to protect the Jedi during this time of crisis.

229 BBY

AZLIN RELL RETURNS
Yoda brings fallen Jedi Azlin Rell to the Council chamber in the Jedi Temple. The other Council members are horrified by Azlin's fall to the dark side, but agree with Yoda that he may be able to help against the Nameless.

229 BBY

SOH'S REQUEST
Chancellor Soh asks for Jedi warriors to aid the Republic Defense Coalition forces who are battling Nihil raiders operating in Republic territory.

The future seems bright for the Jedi Order, the Galactic Republic, and the galaxy at large. Supreme Chancellor Lina Soh works with the Jedi Council to create Great Works, events and construction sites that will bring more worlds into the Republic's fold. However, this period of prosperity is threatened by a band of vicious marauders known as the Nihil. Led by Marchion Ro, this group is determined to sow discord and destruction for its own nefarious reasons.

232 BBY

EMERGENCES
Soh agrees to shut down hyperspace travel after fragments from the *Legacy Run* begin falling from hyperspace across the galaxy. The Republic scrambles to set up a system that can predict where these deadly Emergences will appear.

232 BBY

WAR AGAINST THE NIHIL
After it becomes clear the Nihil are behind the Great Disaster, the Jedi and Galactic Republic vow to defeat them.

232 BBY

BATTLE OF KUR
The Jedi suffer significant losses in a battle with the Nihil near the Kur Nebula.

232 BBY

A NEW KNIGHT
Keeve Trennis is promoted to Jedi Knight on Starlight Beacon by Jedi Master Avar Kriss.

232 BBY

NIHIL SABOTAGE
Jedi Knight Vernestra Rwoh battles the Nihil on Wevo after the ship *Steady Wing* is sabotaged.

232 BBY

DRENGIR THREAT
The Jedi realize their actions have inadvertently released a dangerous carnivorous species, the Drengir, from the ancient Amaxine space station.

232 BBY

KIDNAPPED ON ELPHRONA
On Elphrona, Jedi Master Loden Greatstorm is taken captive by the Nihil.

231 BBY

BATTLE OF GRIZAL
At the Nihil's base on Grizal, Marchion unleashes the Nameless creature known as the Great Leveler against the Jedi. It turns Master Loden Greatstorm to dust.

231 BBY

JEDI INVESTIGATION
Jedi Emerick Caphtor and private detective Sian Holt pair up to investigate Loden's death.

231 BBY

HYPERSPACE MYSTERY
At the Nihil space station Gravity's Heart, captive Mari San Tekka gives Vernestra Rwoh a hyperspace path before she dies.

231 BBY

TAKODANA UNDER FIRE
Jedi Sav Malagán defends the Jedi temple on Takodana from a Nihil raid.

230 BBY

CORELLIA PLOT
Yoda returns to help a group of Jedi foil a Nihil plan to steal Republic ships from Corellia.

230 BBY

DALNA TRAGEDY
Starlight Beacon helps evacuate citizens from Dalna after the Nihil trigger cataclysmic volcano eruptions on the world.

231 BBY

HUNTING THE NIHIL
Keeve Trennis goes undercover as a Nihil captain on Xais. She and fellow Jedi Terec barely escape the Great Leveler.

229 BBY

DISASTER ON TRAVYX PRIME
Yoda and Azlin head to Travyx Prime, a planet with a potential lead regarding the origins of the Nameless. Desperate to destroy all routes to the creatures, Azlin uses the dark side to crash a Republic ship into a city, causing many deaths. He and Yoda witness the event from a nearby shuttle.

229 BBY

A GRIM ANNIVERSARY
To mark a year since the fall of Starlight Beacon, Marchion kills Jedi Council member Pra-Te Veter by setting a Nameless upon him. This brutal execution is broadcast across the galaxy.

CHAPTER ONE

THE JEDI

The rallying cry of the Jedi, "For light and life!" inspires hope in all who hear it. Bonded by the beliefs and actions of the ancient Jedi Order, each Knight pursues their own unique connection with the Force.

PEACEFUL GROWTH

The High Republic is an era of peace for the Jedi. Lightsaber techniques and defensive use of the Force are taught in temples, but no Jedi expects much combat in their lifetime. Jedi believe that they need to keep their emotions in balance, but they are open-minded and accepting of those who choose a different path. The headquarters of the Order is on Coruscant and, as the Republic continues to grow, a number of Jedi outposts are set up throughout the galaxy.

GALACTIC ALLIES

The Jedi work closely with the leaders of the Republic, but neither is beholden to the other. The renowned space station Starlight Beacon, built in partnership between the Republic and the Jedi, reflects what both feel about the galaxy at this time: the future is bright.

THE JEDI

The Jedi Order is the largest and most influential group of Force-sensitive beings in the galaxy. Its members study ancient teachings and train to enhance their connection to the Force. The Order believes that personal attachments, such as romantic relationships, will distract Jedi from their duties.
However, the Jedi are family to one another.

THE LIFE OF A JEDI
Many Jedi come to the Order as younglings. They learn to control the Force through meditation while honing their abilities to perform amazing feats of acrobatics and levitation, bonding with others who do the same. When they are ready, they become Padawans and are paired with an experienced Jedi, who becomes their master.

The master guides them to connect with the Force and instructs them on the role of the Jedi in the galaxy. The bond between master and Padawan becomes one of the most important relationships in a Jedi's life.

GROWING UP

When a Padawan overcomes the challenge of their Jedi Trial, they will become a Jedi Knight. At this point, they cut off their Padawan braid (if they have one) and no longer need to be accompanied by a master. They can choose their own missions and, perhaps, go on to train a Padawan of their own. Knights continue to develop their skills and acquire new knowledge, and, if the Council sees fit, they may eventually go on to attain the rank of Jedi Master.

OTHER PATHS

Being a Jedi isn't only about going on important missions. Some choose to study the writings of those who came before, while others focus on healing, governing, or teaching. Jedi who fall outside the traditional

system still have a place in the Order. Wayseekers follow their own instincts. Though they don't carry out the directions of the Jedi Council, they are still welcomed by it. Some Jedi choose to take the Barash Vow of inaction, cutting themselves off from the rest of the Order and focusing only on their connection to the Force. Some Force users come across the Order later in life. They may be invited to live alongside the Padawans and learn the ways of the Jedi.

THE HIGH COUNCIL

The Jedi Council leads the Order and makes important decisions for its day-to-day direction, and for the future. Chosen for their experience and accomplishments, Council members have the ear of the Republic Senate and chancellor, and are often who the Republic turns to when it needs help. The Jedi do not answer to the Republic, but their hopes for peace and justice often overlap, leading to many collaborative missions, projects, and initiatives that share the same goals.

PORTER ENGLE

THE BLADE OF BARDOTTA

PRONOUNS: He/him
SPECIES: Ikkrukkian
HEIGHT: 1.93 m (6 ft 4 in)

ALLEGIANCE: Jedi Order
FIRST APPEARANCE: LotJ

Porter Engle is one of the most highly regarded duelists in the Jedi Order, whose skills with a lightsaber are unparalleled and admired across the galaxy. In his later years, Porter gains a new reputation as an excellent cook with an easygoing manner. Growing up in the Jedi Temple, he developed a close bond with fellow youngling Barash Silvain.

COUNCIL CONCERN

Porter and Barash are so inseparable that the Jedi Council wants to split them up, concerned about their attachment. However, the younglings hatch a plan. They each concentrate on different skills—Porter on lightsaber combat and telekinesis, and Barash on sensing the energy of the Force and telling truth from lies—making them more powerful as a pair. The two sometimes train separately, but the Council never forces them apart.

BATTLE ON GANSEVOR

Under siege, the envoy of the planet Gansevor sends out a call for help to the Jedi, and Porter and Barash answer. Porter is determined to save lives while there, and is adamant that he won't kill or be used as a soldier in someone else's war.

When a battle breaks out, Barash shows her trust in the Force and Porter as she walks through a rain of blaster fire without fear because she knows Porter has her back.

Beard wraps inspired by Barash's braids

"NO ONE SHOULD BE HUNGRY."

– Porter Engle

Almost single-handedly, Porter takes on the mercenary General Viess and her army. The Jedi is careful not to kill, instead making blasters leap out of people's hands, even when they intend to use full force against him. Porter's lightsaber blade moves quickly and precisely, cutting at the weaker material that holds Viess' beskar armor together. Viess can't gain the upper hand, so she throws an explosive into the crowd, knowing Porter will abandon their duel to save the lives of others. While Porter does just as she predicted, Viess uses the moment to flee.

COOKING IN THE WILDERNESS

Porter withdraws from frontline combat after experiencing a devastating trauma. Later in his long Ikkrukkian life, he enjoys cooking at a Jedi outpost on Elphrona. He continues to use his lightsaber skills, though he is more likely to be found slicing ingredients for a new dish than dueling.

MEMORIES FROM LONG AGO

Porter later rejoins the Jedi on the front lines and, during the Nihil attack on Valo, uses a form of battle meditation to unite the minds of other Jedi to fly their starships in formation with his. He later shares memories of his eventful past, including recollections of his time as the legendary "Blade of Bardotta."

Flexible leather boots support Porter's large frame

VILDAR MAC

HAUNTED JEDI KNIGHT

PRONOUNS: He/him
SPECIES: Kiffar
HEIGHT: 1.91 m (6 ft 3 in)

ALLEGIANCE: Jedi Order
FIRST APPEARANCE: THR (PII)

Vildar Mac is a gruff, serious Jedi Master who is sent on assignment to the Holy City on Jedha, where he works alongside Padawan Matthea Cathley. The duo investigate one of the many relics that have recently gone missing in the city. Vildar is surprised to learn that many civilians on Jedha do not have favorable opinions of the Jedi. He uses Force visions to help during his missions, but the visions are hard to control and take a large toll on him.

TRAUMATIC PAST

Vildar is haunted by a childhood memory from before he joined the Jedi Order. As a four-year-old, he witnessed a stranger—one of the Sorcerers of Tund—kill several people in his village on Kiffex. Vildar felt a darkness from this evildoer that he never forgot. Years later, Jedi Master Larti saved Vildar, and took him as his Padawan.

TROUBLES ON JEDHA

Vildar panics when he sees the Sorcerer of Tund Tarna Miak in the streets of Jedha—he fears Miak will be as dangerous as the villain who terrified him as a child. Later, the Herald of the Path of the Open Hand causes a riot on the steps of the Convocation of the Force, and Vildar is overcome with terror and confusion when a Nameless creature is unleashed in the Holy City.

> "I DON'T NEED RESPECT—
> I ONLY NEED THE FORCE."
>
> – Vildar Mac

UNLIKELY ALLIES

Vildar is at first frustrated and irritated by the eccentric Tey Sirrek, who is also investigating the stolen relics on Jedha. Yet Vildar and Tey soon form a close bond. Vildar questions whether the Guardians of the Whills are unfairly blaming Sirrek for recent thefts, and Sirrek comes to Vildar's aid when he is trapped under a building during the Battle of Jedha. When Vildar believes Sirrek has been killed by the Path of the Open Hand, he renounces the light side of the Force and momentarily touches the dark side. After the battle, Vildar takes up a position on the Convocation and asks Sirrek to join him.

Facial tattoo acquired as a child

Reinforced gloves

BARASH SILVAIN

TRUTH-TELLER

Tunic allows for acrobatic movement

Belt pouches hold emergency survival gear

PRONOUNS: She/her
SPECIES: Kage
HEIGHT: 1.80 m (5 ft 11 in)

ALLEGIANCE: Jedi Order
FIRST APPEARANCE: THR: TB

Barash Silvain grows up in the Jedi Temple with Porter Engle. As younglings, the two are as close as siblings. Unlike most Jedi, Barash's superb memory allows her to recall her birth family perfectly, even though she was just an infant when she was taken to join the Order.

THE BARASH VOW

Barash's ability to sense the truth fails her years later on Gansevor. She is betrayed by Princess Sicatra, who plays on Barash's emotions. Devastated, Barash vows to remain a Jedi but to never again take action on behalf of the Order. Long after Barash's death, some Jedi continue to honor her act, which becomes known as the Barash Vow.

"VIOLENCE IS ALWAYS THE JEDI'S LAST RESORT."

– Barash Silvain

MATTHEA CATHLEY

TALKATIVE JEDI PADAWAN

Protective headpiece

Fingerless gloves enable a firm grip on her lightsaber

PRONOUNS: She/her
SPECIES: Twi'lek
HEIGHT: 1.68 m (5 ft 6 in)

ALLEGIANCE: Jedi Order, Convocation of the Force
FIRST APPEARANCE: THR (PII)

Matthea Cathley, also known as Matty, is a confident, enthusiastic Padawan stationed on Jedha, where her master, Leebon, represents the Jedi to the Convocation of the Force. Matty is an excellent peacekeeper, and her patience and goodwill are welcome qualities on the turbulent moon. She helps explain to those outside the Jedi Order that the Jedi are on Jedha to advise and mediate—not promote their own views.

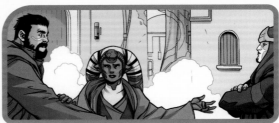

SECRET MISSION

Matty works alongside Leebon's aide, Jedi Oliviah Zeveron, though the two are not close friends. After the Battle of Jedha, Matty and Oliviah head to Dalna to learn more about the Path of the Open Hand. There, Matty stops Jedi Knight Azlin Rell from using the Force to choke the Path's second-in-command, the Herald.

"IT'S WHAT THE CONVOCATION IS ALL ABOUT. OPENING DIALOGUE BETWEEN BELIEVERS."
— Matthea Cathley

SAV MALAGÁN

PIRATE JEDI

Kyuzo war shield hat

PRONOUNS: She/her
SPECIES: Kyuzo
HEIGHT: 1.65 m (5 ft 5 in)

ALLEGIANCE: Jedi Order, Maz's crew
FIRST APPEARANCE: THRA (PI)

Bored with meditation lessons and lightsaber training, Padawan Sav Malagán seeks adventure. She sneaks away from the Takodana Jedi temple at night, heading to Maz Kanata's castle, where she joins up with Maz and her crew on their exciting exploits. These include an undercover mission with the Dank Graks criminal group and a close-up view of the Battle of Jedha.

FIGHTING THE NIHIL

As a master many years later, Malagán is the lone Jedi guarding the Takodana temple when Nihil cell leader Krix Kamerat attacks. Malagán remains calm and focused, defeating the Nihil ships with her dual purple lightsaber and sending Krix back in defeat.

"WHAT'S THE POINT OF BEING ABLE TO USE THE FORCE... IF YOU'RE NOT GOING TO CAUSE A LITTLE TROUBLE WITH IT?"

– Sav Malagán

GELLA NATTAI

JEDI KNIGHT WAYSEEKER

Jedi symbol

PRONOUNS: She/her
SPECIES: Human
HEIGHT: 1.63 m (5 ft 4 in)

ALLEGIANCE: Jedi Order
FIRST APPEARANCE: Con

Curious, intuitive, and at times impulsive, Jedi Knight Gella Nattai seeks to understand her place in the galaxy. During a mission to deliver medical supplies, Gella finds herself at the center of a ceasefire about to fall apart between warring planets Eiram and E'ronoh. After helping to keep the peace, she petitions the Jedi Council to become a Wayseeker so she can follow her own path.

> "FIGHT, UNTIL YOU CANNOT FIGHT ANY MORE. FOR LIFE. FOR LIGHT. FOR ALL OF US."
>
> – Gella Nattai

THE JEDI AND THE SCOUNDREL

Gella is intrigued and frustrated by Axel Greylark, the charming son of Chancellor Kyong Greylark, when he joins her mission on Eiram. Despite Axel's faults and selfish behavior, Gella sees his potential and tries to change his negative feelings about the Jedi. Over time, she also grows concerned at how she seems to behave more impulsively in his presence, and is more driven by her feelings.

CREIGHTON SUN

BURDENED JEDI MASTER

Crossguard lightsaber based on an ancient design

PRONOUNS: He/him
SPECIES: Human
HEIGHT: 1.83 m (6 ft)

ALLEGIANCE: Jedi Order
FIRST APPEARANCE: Con

Creighton Sun is a calm and practical Jedi Master. Although he can seem grumpy, and prefers solitary work to social events, he is good at handling even the most difficult of conversations. Creighton travels to Eiram and E'ronoh, and then Dalna during the Path of the Open Hand crisis.

PEACE WITHIN A WAR

Creighton is on Jedha during the signing of the Eiram–E'ronoh peace-treaty. He attempts to discover who is behind the attacks on it. When battle threatens to break out, he uses his negotiation skills to talk down the soldiers, reminding them that by initiating violence they've already lost. Later, Creighton and several other Jedi clash with the Path of the Open Hand at its compound on Dalna. Creighton only narrowly survives.

"THE NEW GENERATION WILL LEAD THE OLD TOWARD A BETTER FUTURE."
— Creighton Sun

AIDA FORTE

OPTIMISTIC JEDI KNIGHT

Scales adapt to desert sand and heat

Lightsaber hilt holds green kyber crystal

PRONOUNS: She/her
SPECIES: Kadas'sa'Nikto
HEIGHT: 1.68 m (5 ft 6 in)

ALLEGIANCE: Jedi Order
FIRST APPEARANCE: Con

Aida Forte is a devout Jedi Knight who believes strongly in the light side of the Force. She encourages others to have faith that future events will go in their favor. She often works alongside Master Creighton Sun, and is a positive voice beside his more jaded attitude. Aida is confident in her hopes that the warring planets Eiram and E'ronoh will make peace someday.

LAST BATTLE
Aida sneaks into the Path of the Open Hand compound on Dalna, along with fellow Jedi Yaddle, Creighton, and Cippa Tarko. Both Aida and Creighton fight back when the Path sends its droids to attack them and the local townspeople. Yaddle pulls Aida from the clash, but it is too late—Aida is fatally injured.

"WAR CASTS A LONG SHADOW."

– Aida Forte

SILANDRA SHO

PEACEFUL JEDI MASTER

Sheets of plasma appear when shield is activated

Blue-bladed lightsaber

PRONOUNS: She/her
SPECIES: Human
HEIGHT: 1.78 m (5 ft 10 in)

ALLEGIANCE: Jedi Order
FIRST APPEARANCE: QftHC

Master Silandra Sho sees herself more as a protector than a fighter. She keeps an open mind as she leads a Republic Pathfinder team across the frontier. Quiet, focused, and thoughtful, Silandra embraces her role as teacher and mentor to her Padawan, Rooper Nitani, and she later gifts Rooper her shield when the Padawan becomes a Jedi Knight.

SIGNS OF THINGS TO COME

On the moon of Jedha, Jedi Master Creighton Sun asks Silandra to investigate the bombing that has disrupted a peace treaty between the planets Eiram and E'ronoh. After more violence erupts, Silandra becomes suspicious of the Mother of the Path of the Open Hand. She also grows alarmed by her brief encounter with a mysterious creature she believes altered her connection to the Force.

"PATHFINDERS ARE RESOURCEFUL. IT'S IN OUR NATURE."

— Silandra Sho

ROOPER NITANI

ADVENTUROUS JEDI PADAWAN

Rooper uses twin blue lightsabers

Pockets for extra supplies on the frontier

PRONOUNS: She/her
SPECIES: Human
HEIGHT: 1.57 m (5 ft 2 in)

ALLEGIANCE: Jedi Order
FIRST APPEARANCE: QftHC

Padawan Rooper Nitani has the rare ability to see the Force as colors. She joins her Jedi Master, Silandra Sho, on an Outer Rim Pathfinder team. Rooper is eager to prove herself to Master Sho and she does so by protecting a rare salmaca creature during her Jedi Trial on Batuu. Rooper is excited to explore the galaxy and help people.

DIFFERENT PERSPECTIVES

Rooper strongly believes in the Jedi and has tremendous respect for her master's ability to resolve conflicts peacefully. When Rooper unexpectedly finds herself taking part in the Hyperspace Chase with explorer Dass Leffbruk and pilot Sky Graf, she is surprised to discover the controversial views of the Force held by the Path of the Open Hand.

"I WANT TO SERVE THE FORCE.
HELP BRING LIGHT TO THE GALAXY,
ESPECIALLY OUT HERE."

– Rooper Nitani

ROK BURAN

RUGGED FRONTIER JEDI

Scars tell of many dangerous adventures

Custom-built dagger is useful on expeditions and handy for whittling

Mission attire

PRONOUNS: He/him
SPECIES: Human
HEIGHT: 1.75 m (5 ft 9 in)

ALLEGIANCE: Jedi Order
FIRST APPEARANCE: QftHC

More comfortable on frontier worlds than on Coruscant, Master Rok Buran is one of the most experienced Jedi working in the Outer Rim. Rok and his Pathfinder team run into trouble on Aubadas when they answer a call for help from the local Katikoot population. The team is attacked by monsters, and Rok is devastated to discover that he is the only survivor, having lost his Padawan, Maliq, as well as the rest of the team.

A NEW PADAWAN
On another mission, Rok is once again stranded on a remote planet. He teams up with Padawan Coron Solstus, encouraging the young man to embrace the adventure of being a frontier Jedi. When Coron's master dies, Rok takes him as his new Padawan.

"I SURVIVED. BARELY. AND THAT'S ALL I'VE BEEN DOING IN THE DAYS SINCE. SURVIVING."

– Rok Buran

30

OLIVIAH ZEVERON

DETERMINED JEDI KNIGHT

Battle-ready stance

Leather boots from Sullust

PRONOUNS: She/her
SPECIES: Human
HEIGHT: 1.63 m (5 ft 4 in)

ALLEGIANCE: Jedi Order, Convocation of the Force
FIRST APPEARANCE: THR (PII)

Oliviah Zeveron is the aide to Master Leebon, the Jedi representative in the Convocation of the Force. Oliviah mainly keeps to herself, seeking time alone in the desert outside Jedha to meditate. She grows frustrated by the politics within the Convocation and sometimes regrets she did not choose a path that would allow her to travel the galaxy.

FAMILY REUNION
Oliviah travels to Dalna with Padawan Matty Cathley to investigate the odd feelings she had in the presence of the Mother of the Open Hand. When Oliviah and the Mother come face to face, Oliviah remembers the moment when, as a child, she was selected to join the Jedi. The Mother, known back then as Elecia Zeveron, is Oliviah's sister, and was not chosen to train as a Jedi.

"I DON'T KNOW WHAT I'M FOLLOWING HERE, WHERE THE FORCE IS LEADING ME."
– Oliviah Zeveron

AZLIN RELL

TROUBLED JEDI KNIGHT

Weatherproof
mission robes

PRONOUNS: He/him
SPECIES: Human
HEIGHT: 1.70 m (5 ft 7 in)

ALLEGIANCE: Jedi Order
FIRST APPEARANCE: MH

Jedi Knight Azlin Rell is sent to investigate the disappearance of fellow Jedi Zallah Macri and Kevmo Zink. His mission leads him to Dalna, where he is affected by the Nameless and terrified by dark visions that overwhelm him. This experience sets Azlin on a dangerous path to learn everything he can about the Nameless, including how to destroy them.

SECRETS FROM THE PAST

Azlin becomes obsessed with exploring the fear caused by the Nameless. He studies obscure dark-side teachings, which unexpectedly extend his life span. His unusually

long life means he is still alive 150 years later, when Yoda seeks him out. The Jedi Council wants to welcome Azlin back to the Order, though they have some concerns over how much he has lost his way.

"THE HALLUCINATIONS STILL HAUNT ME."

– Azlin Rell

YADDLE

POWERFUL AND SUBTLE JEDI

PRONOUNS: She/her
SPECIES: Unknown
HEIGHT: 61 cm (2 ft)

ALLEGIANCE: Jedi Order
FIRST APPEARANCE: OotS

Simple, traditional wrappings

Shoto lightsaber matches her natural height

Master Yaddle sits on the Jedi Council and knows the ins and outs of how to educate younglings. She doesn't believe in teaching unquestioning optimism—instead, she encourages them to accept whatever the Force brings. Yaddle offers her advice to new students at the Jedi Temple with patience and compassion. When a young Vernestra Rwoh comes to the Temple, Yaddle teaches Vernestra her first lesson—to trust her instincts.

"I DO NOT FIGHT UNLESS IT IS ABSOLUTELY NECESSARY."

– Yaddle

CLASH ON DALNA

Although she isn't officially assigned there, Yaddle travels to Dalna to help battle the Path of the Open Hand. Yaddle only fights as a last resort, but she and others within the Order, including Aida Forte and Yoda, present a strong Jedi front against the cult. Yaddle pushes the Path back by deflecting blaster bolts and throwing people into the air with the Force, buying the other Jedi time when they most need it. She also guides the youngling Cippa Tarko in battle.

CHAR-RYL-ROY

RELIABLE JEDI MASTER

Lightsaber houses a yellow kyber crystal

PRONOUNS: He/him
SPECIES: Cerean
HEIGHT: 1.98 m (6 ft 6 in)

ALLEGIANCE: Jedi Order
FIRST APPEARANCE: Con

Jedi Master Char-Ryl-Roy is a good listener and always tries to see both sides in every situation. This leads him to make rational decisions, though he is known for overthinking at times. He trains Padawan Enya Keen, but his lessons sometimes frustrate her, for example when he gives her the wrong droid repair parts to prove she needs to understand "the limits of what's possible."

SHOWDOWN ON DALNA
Along with Enya and Princess Xiri A'lbaran of E'ronoh, Char-Ryl-Roy attempts to negotiate with the Path of the Open Hand on Dalna. However, the Path's compound erupts into conflict, and he and Enya gather Republic supporters for the fight. In the end, Char-Ryl-Roy loses his life to the Nameless creature known as the Leveler.

"ALL JEDI TO ME!"
– Char-Ryl-Roy

ENYA KEEN

CURIOUS PADAWAN

PRONOUNS: She/her
SPECIES: Human
HEIGHT: 1.68 m (5 ft 6 in)

ALLEGIANCE: Jedi Order
FIRST APPEARANCE: Con

Enya Keen is an irreverent and curious Jedi. She trains under Master Char-Ryl-Roy and sees the Force as a blowing wind. Enya is talented at building and repairing droids, and can usually be found tinkering with something mechanical. There's an emotional side to her desire to repair droids, too—her heart goes out to suffering beings. Enya firmly believes in the Jedi and Republic's mission to promote galactic peace, wholeheartedly agreeing with Master Yoda's plan to send her to the warring planets Eiram and E'ronoh.

THE BATTLE OF DALNA
Enya and Master Char-Ryl-Roy fight against the Path of the Open Hand on Dalna. After Char-Ryl-Roy's tragic death, Enya takes his lightsaber's kyber crystal in his memory. With it, she builds a second lightsaber for herself.

"A JEDI IS NEVER LOST."

– Enya Keen

CIPPA TARKO

PRONOUNS: She/her
SPECIES: Arkanian
HEIGHT: 69 cm (2 ft 3 in)

ALLEGIANCE: Jedi Order
FIRST APPEARANCE: Cat

Force-sensitive child Cippa Tarko is discovered by Jedi Master Yaddle. However, instead of taking her to the Temple on Coruscant, Yaddle takes Cippa to Dalna, where the Jedi are facing off against the Path of the Open Hand. Cippa has little fear of the battle. She's impatient, confident, and knows she's gifted with the Force. She easily overpowers the Republic guards sent to keep her away from the fighting and joins in. Cippa breaks a Path Member's blaster, but is injured in the fray. Republic guard Priv Ittik steps up to protect her.

"I BROKE THAT BLASTER BEFORE WE LEFT. THAT WEAPON WON'T EVER BE USED BY A CHILD LIKE ME."

– Cippa Tarko, after taking a blaster from a Path member

ELA SUTAN

PRONOUNS: She/her
SPECIES: Caamasi
HEIGHT: 1.75 m (5 ft 9 in)

ALLEGIANCE: Jedi Order
FIRST APPEARANCE: Yod

Ela Sutan sits on the Jedi Council. She is one of the older members, having been appointed to the role even before fellow Master Pra-Tre Veter. Sutan works with Pra-Tre regularly, but often disagrees with him. She worries that the Council sometimes loses sight of its core Jedi belief that all life is precious. When the Scalvi people of the planet Turrak send a distress call to the Council, Pra-Tre questions whether it is the Jedi's duty to respond personally. Sutan emphasizes the importance of the Scalvi message, pointing out that no Council business is more important than helping people in need.

"ALL LIFE IS LUMINOUS."

– Ela Sutan

XINITH TARL

PRONOUNS: She/her
ALLEGIANCE: Jedi Order
SPECIES: Bith
FIRST APPEARANCE: TBoJ
HEIGHT: 1.80 m (5 ft 11 in)

Bith are known for their excellent hearing

As a member of the Jedi Council, Xinith Tarl is at the epicenter of a growing Republic. Tarl is always quick to offer support to other Jedi. She agrees to send help to Jedha after receiving a distress call from Creighton Sun. She also counsels Rok Buran that he should not blame himself for the loss of his Padawan, Maliq, suggesting instead that he takes time for reflection. Tarl has the rare ability to stay calm during a crisis. She refuses to give up hope even when she is gravely injured on a remote planet while on board the Pathfinder ship *Witherbloom*.

"THIS IS THE REPUBLIC PATHFINDER VESSEL *WITHERBLOOM*. DO YOU REQUIRE ASSISTANCE?"

– Xinith Tarl

RAVNA ABRONSA

PRONOUNS: She/her
ALLEGIANCE: Jedi Order
SPECIES: Human
FIRST APPEARANCE: TEoB: P
HEIGHT: 1.57 m (5 ft 2 in)

Jedi Master Ravna Abronsa thinks carefully before entering into combat. She knows that often, in times of conflict, patience and precision are more important than brute strength. She teaches Arkoff, her former Padawan, to use the same calculated approach during the Battle of Dalna. After coming to the aid of Jedi Knight Azlin Rell, who is under attack from the soldiers of the Path of the Open Hand, Abronsa orders Azlin and Arkoff to fall back, saving their lives. When Abronsa senses a disturbance in the Force, she investigates but, despite her cautious nature, is killed by a Nameless creature.

Hood often worn during moments of reflection

KEVMO ZINK

PRONOUNS: He/him
SPECIES: Pantoran
HEIGHT: 1.78 m (5 ft 10 in)

ALLEGIANCE: Jedi Order
FIRST APPEARANCE: PoD

When enthusiastic Jedi Kevmo Zink meets Marda Ro, a member of the Path of the Open Hand, the two fall in love despite their opposing philosophies about the Force. Kevmo helps Marda save fellow Path members from a flood, and is tempted to stay and build a life with her. However, he eventually tells her they can't be together due to the Jedi principle of nonattachment. Kevmo and his Jedi Master, Zallah Macri, later become suspicious that the cult's leader, the Mother, might be stealing Force artifacts. When they go to investigate, the Mother and her second-in-command, the Herald, fight back and release a Nameless creature.

Uses the Force easily and joyfully

Lightsaber used to see in the dark and as a weapon

ZALLAH MACRI

PRONOUNS: She/her
SPECIES: Soikan
HEIGHT: 1.80 m (5 ft 11 in)

ALLEGIANCE: Jedi Order
FIRST APPEARANCE: PoD

Dignified and averse to touch, Zallah Macri is in many ways the opposite of her Padawan, Kevmo Zink. They are assigned to search for a stolen artifact, and rumors lead them to the planet Dalna. There, Zallah learns about the Path of the Open Hand. She investigates the cult cautiously and warns Kevmo not to give in to attachment when he develops a connection with Path member Marda Ro. Zallah and Kevmo confront the group's leader, the Mother, but Zallah's Force abilities are no match for the creature the Mother controls.

BARNABAS VIM

PRONOUNS: He/him
SPECIES: Human
HEIGHT: 1.78 m (5 ft 10 in)

ALLEGIANCE: Jedi Order
FIRST APPEARANCE: THRA: QotJ

Jedi Master Barnabas Vim is a wise mystic who is sometimes considered a loner. There are times where his meditation looks like idleness or sleep but, as he tells his Padawan, Vix Fonnick, the "wisdom of the dreaming mind" can unlock secrets the conscious mind can't. Vim and Fonnick travel to the planet Angcord to discover the nature of the Echo Stone, an artifact imbued with the Force. While meditating Vim has a vision, revealing that the stone's dark side is draining the planet of life. He vows to discover the origins of the stone.

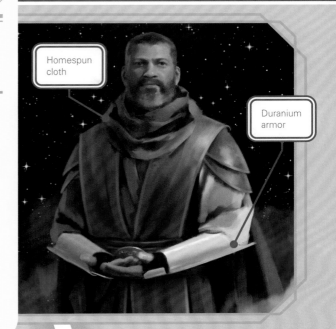

Homespun cloth

Duranium armor

VIX FONNICK

PRONOUNS: She/her
SPECIES: Twi'lek
HEIGHT: 1.68 m (5 ft 6 in)

ALLEGIANCE: Jedi Order
FIRST APPEARANCE: THRA: QotJ

Vix Fonnick is still learning to follow in Master Barnabas Vim's footsteps. She sometimes acts without thinking, and can be inquisitive and alert almost to the point of being on edge. More expressive and quicker to fight than her master, Fonnick is still learning to control her emotions. During their mission to Angcord, she steps up to protect Vim from the royal guard, known as Pilgrim Warriors, but he tells her to stand down. Her quick reactions serve her well on other occasions, though. She acts swiftly to cut the Echo Stone into pieces, ending its dark-side influence before it does too much damage.

Decorative lekku wrap

Lightsaber built with Master Vim's help

" 'LEGEND SAYS'? WHY DIDN'T WE JUST CALL AHEAD AND CHECK?"

– Vix Fonnick

SULA BADANI

PRONOUNS: She/her
SPECIES: Human
HEIGHT: 1.65 m (5 ft 5 in)

ALLEGIANCE: Jedi Order
FIRST APPEARANCE:
THRA: TNT

Jedi Master Sula Badani flies on board the Pathfinder ship *Witherbloom* with her Padawan, Coron Solstus. Badani is patient with Coron, helping ease his anxiety when they crash on a remote planet. After fighting off several Path of the Open Hand members, who are also stranded there, Badani is almost overcome by the Nameless creatures they are transporting. Later, she sacrifices her life for her team.

CORON SOLSTUS

PRONOUNS: He/him
SPECIES: Human
HEIGHT: 1.68 m (5 ft 6 in)

ALLEGIANCE: Jedi Order
FIRST APPEARANCE:
THRA: TNT

Eager Padawan Coron Solstus joins his master, Sula Badani, on the Pathfinder team. Coron's combat skills are put to the test when the ship crashes alongside a Path of the Open Hand ship. Jedi Master Rok Buran and Coron explore the Path ship, hoping to offer help to its passengers, but are both overcome by the Nameless on board until Master Badani helps them all escape.

ORIN DARHGA

PRONOUNS: He/him
SPECIES: Human
HEIGHT: 1.73 m (5 ft 8 in)

ALLEGIANCE: Jedi Order
FIRST APPEARANCE: Cat

Jedi Master Orin Darhga is an optimist, even under the most dire circumstances. When he and Jedi Knight Gella Nattai are in pursuit of Axel Greylark and the Path of the Open Hand, Darhga switches between reassuring Gella and telling jokes. Like Gella, Darhga is very intuitive and can sense when people are lying—even when they are lying to themselves.

"EVEN FELLOW JEDI WITH PURE MINDS AND HEARTS NEED GUIDANCE."

– Orin Darhga

HAR'KIN

PRONOUNS: He/him
SPECIES: Gran
HEIGHT: 1.75 m (5 ft 9 in)

ALLEGIANCE: Jedi Order
FIRST APPEARANCE: TBoJ

Jedi Master Har'kin arrives toward the end of the Battle of Jedha. He reports that Republic troops will immediately begin a relief effort in the city. He also insists that Jedi Creighton Sun and Aida Forte take time to rest and recover from their harrowing experiences.

"YOU NEED TIME TO MEDITATE. TO COMMUNE WITH THE FORCE. TO COME TO TERMS WITH WHAT YOU'VE WITNESSED."

– Har'kin

HELION VOLTE

PRONOUNS: They/them
SPECIES: Mikkian
HEIGHT: 1.83 m (6 ft)

ALLEGIANCE: Jedi Order, Galactic Republic
FIRST APPEARANCE: THR: TB

Helion Volte leads Pathfinder team 807, which aims to expand the Republic comms network. Volte was one of the best in their class at lightsaber dueling, but they can't defeat Jedi Porter Engle, a passenger on their Pathfinder ship, in a practice duel.

BENJ MARKO

PRONOUNS: He/him
SPECIES: Human
HEIGHT: 1.68 m (5 ft 6 in)

ALLEGIANCE: Jedi Order, Galactic Republic
FIRST APPEARANCE: THR: TB

Benj Marko trains with his Jedi Master, Helion Volte, during their voyages as part of a Republic Pathfinder team. Their primary mission is to set up new Republic communications nodes. Benj watches Volte and Porter Engle practice dueling, and protests when Volte says that Benj isn't yet skilled enough to practice dueling against them.

LEE HARRO

PRONOUNS: He/him
SPECIES: Human
HEIGHT: 1.70 m (5 ft 7 in)

ALLEGIANCE: Jedi Order
FIRST APPEARANCE: ToE: LO

Lee Harro is an easygoing Jedi whose relaxed attitude makes him a good fit for frontier exploration. He can come off as aloof and unfocused, but he's deeply at peace with himself and always happy to go with the flow. He shares an adventure on a pirate starship with hyperspace prospector Saretha von Beel, before heading to the planet Vexos with her.

KAKTORF

PRONOUNS: He/him
SPECIES: Unknown
HEIGHT: 1.98 m (6 ft 6 in)

ALLEGIANCE: Jedi Order
FIRST APPEARANCE: THRA (PII)

Kaktorf trains the Padawan Sav Malagán at the Takodana temple. He's strict, insisting Sav not stay out past curfew and scolding her for running off with Maz and her crew. Malagán remembers Kaktorf as a wise master, though prone to what she considers micromanaging.

"I STILL DON'T UNDERSTAND WHAT YOU WERE DOING OUT PAST CURFEW IN THE FIRST PLACE, MY PADAWAN!"

– Kaktorf

LEEBON

JEDI CONVOCATION REPRESENTATIVE

Some Selonians' eyes are sensitive to bright lights

Protective robes for desert climate

PRONOUNS: She/her
SPECIES: Selonian
HEIGHT: 1.75 m (5 ft 9 in)

ALLEGIANCE: Jedi Order, Convocation of the Force
FIRST APPEARANCE: THR (PII)

Jedi Master Leebon represents the Jedi Order in the Convocation of the Force on Jedha. Along with her Padawan, Matthea Cathley, and her aide, Oliviah Zeveron, Leebon works with other Convocation members to find common ground. Leebon is keenly aware that her role within the Convocation is to abide by the consensus of the group, rather than interfering in local matters.

SENSE OF CONVICTION

Leebon encourages her fellow Jedi and Convocation members to stay calm after a bombing at the Temple of the Kyber, but she'll also speak her mind when needed. She strongly refutes the Herald of the Path of the Open Hand when he claims that using the Force does others harm.

> "WITH ALL DUE RESPECT, HERALD, THAT IS NOT HOW THE FORCE OPERATES."
>
> – Leebon

ADY SUN'ZEE

MIRIALAN JEDI KNIGHT

Pouch to carry artifacts

PRONOUNS: She/her
SPECIES: Mirialan
HEIGHT: 1.73 m (5 ft 8 in)

ALLEGIANCE: Jedi Order
FIRST APPEARANCE: TfGE

As a Padawan, Ady Sun'Zee studies ancient artifacts at a Jedi research outpost on Batuu with her Jedi Master, Sylwin. One artifact exerts its dark-side influence, overwhelming Sylwin and Ady. Ady struggles against the corruptive power until support arrives in the form of Jedi Master Yoda. Together, they seal away the dangerous object. Yoda is impressed by Ady's courage, and Ady eventually rises to the rank of Jedi Knight and takes on her own Padawan, Nooa.

FULL CIRCLE
Ady never forgets Master Sylwin, and she uses Sylwin's kyber crystal to power her own lightsaber. When Ady decides it's time to move on, she takes Nooa to Valron—a place Ady and Sylwin visited together—and returns the crystal.

Weather-resistant boots

"NOT ALL CHALLENGES ARE OPPONENTS, PADAWAN."

– Ady Sun'Zee

YODA

LEGENDARY GRAND MASTER

PRONOUNS: He/him
SPECIES: Unknown
HEIGHT: 66 cm (2 ft 2 in)

ALLEGIANCE: Jedi Order
FIRST APPEARANCE: LotJ

He lets himself be captured to test what a young Scalvi, Bree, will do when faced with violence. Bree kills a Crulkon, failing the test. Yoda leaves Turrak for the length of a Scalvi generation, and returns when Bree is an adult. This time, Bree understands what Yoda was trying to show him years ago—the Crulkon were starving and desperate. Bree makes peace, and Yoda asks the Jedi to send an environmental team to find out why the fish the Crulkon survived on disappeared.

Grand Master Yoda has been training young Jedi with his signature combination of mischievousness and mystery for hundreds of years. He rarely says exactly what he's thinking, preferring to hint and guide his students—allowing them to make mistakes so they can figure out his lessons on their own.

AN IMPORTANT LESSON

Yoda sometimes goes on missions for long periods of time. After he receives a distress call from the planet Turrak, he spends months there despite the other Council members wanting him to come back. The Scalvi people of Turrak are being attacked by Crulkon raiders. Yoda teaches the Scalvi to build defenses while advising them not to become aggressors.

WISE MENTOR

Yoda is still on the Jedi Council 150 years later. He's trained a lot of Jedi over the years, including his Padawan Kantam Sy, against whom he often practices dueling. When Kantam considers leaving the Jedi Order to build a life with their partner, Yoda listens to their concerns and lets them depart. Years later, Yoda welcomes Kantam back to the Order and names them a Jedi Knight.

Gimer wood cane

"SERVE THE LIGHT. SERVE LIFE."

– Yoda

LIFETIME OF SERVICE

Yoda takes a break from Coruscant to train younglings on board the starship academy *Star Hopper*. The ship diverts from its usual course to respond to a call for help in the Trymant system. There, Yoda clashes with Marchion Ro and the Nihil. He also recruits Zeen Mrala, a Force-sensitive girl, to help the Jedi on board the space station Starlight Beacon. Yoda later encounters Elder Tromak, an Elder of the Path of the Open Hand cult, who had been present when the Path finally fell.

ANCIENT SECRETS

Yoda stands alongside Grand Master Pra-Tre Veter as he offers Jedi Master Avar Kriss the role of Marshal of Starlight Beacon. Sometime before the fall of the space station, Yoda goes on another mysterious journey where he aims to learn more about the past to help save people in the present.

YODA'S RETURN

When the Nihil attack Corellia, Yoda fights alongside Kantam Sy, Reath Silas, Zeen Mrala, Cohmac Vitus, and Ram Jomaram. Afterward, Yoda joins Cohmac and Kantam in awarding Reath the rank of Jedi Knight. When Cohmac declares he's decided to leave the Order, Yoda lets him go with a nod.

KEEVE TRENNIS

BOLD JEDI KNIGHT

PRONOUNS: She/her
SPECIES: Human
HEIGHT: 1.68 m (5 ft 6 in)

ALLEGIANCE: Jedi Order
FIRST APPEARANCE: AToC

Things don't always go as planned for passionate and determined Jedi Keeve Trennis, but that doesn't stop her from forging her way through difficult situations. Keeve sometimes doubts herself, yet she's a born leader and a loyal friend to her fellow Jedi. Able to sense when things are amiss, Keeve will do all she can to protect those in need, and she regularly finds unique solutions to conflicts.

JEDI TRIALS

Keeve's Jedi Trials do not go as she'd expected. Tasked with retrieving an artifact known as a Tythonian pendant, Keeve is interrupted by a swarm of destructive star-locusts. She quickly adapts and helps divert them back to their original path through space. Keeve's smart ideas stop the locusts from causing more damage, and prove her readiness to be a Jedi Knight.

MIND GAMES

As a Jedi Knight, Keeve takes great risks to protect others from the carnivorous, plantlike Drengir. On the planet Sedri Minor, she discovers that her former master, Sskeer, is under Drengir influence. Keeve uses a mind touch to slow the Drengir down, and she even joins Sskeer inside the Drengir's root-mind, at great personal cost. She helps the Jedi find the source Drengir, the Great Progenitor, on the planet Mulita. Keeve agrees to let herself be infected by the Drengir to see if there's a way to stop them for good.

Mission attire

"NOT TODAY. NOT WHILE OUR SABERS BURN."

— Keeve Trennis

NOT BACKING DOWN

While Keeve is in awe of the Jedi Knights and Masters on Starlight Beacon, she doesn't shy away from arguing with them, presenting a different point of view or disobeying their orders completely. Keeve refuses to believe Sskeer's value to the Jedi is lost, even when she learns of his serious condition. She also stands up to Avar Kriss in No-Space when she sees that Kriss' desire for revenge against Lourna Dee and the Nihil has clouded her judgment. Keeve helps steer Kriss back to the light, reminding her that mercy is a strength rather than a weakness of the Jedi. Keeve's bravery and fierce loyalty to her friends quickly cast her as a Jedi Knight others can trust and look up to.

Double-bladed lightsaber can be split into two single blade sabers

STELLAN GIOS

THE JEDI'S GUIDING STAR

PRONOUNS: He/him
SPECIES: Human
HEIGHT: 1.80 m (5 ft 11 in)

ALLEGIANCE: Jedi Order
FIRST APPEARANCE: LotJ

Master Stellan Gios is a firm believer in the traditions of the Jedi Order. He sits on the Jedi Council, offering leadership and guidance in the uncertain times following the Nihil attacks. Along with his friends, Avar Kriss and Elzar Mann, Stellan is one of the foremost Jedi Masters of his age. He considers his group of friends as a constellation of three stars.

STELLAR RISE

Stellan is an accomplished Jedi, but during his training he sometimes struggled, unlike Avar and Elzar. As a Padawan under Master Rana Kant, Stellan wasn't always so devout, often getting in trouble along with his friends. Later, as a Jedi Master himself, Stellan befriends and trains the confident and talented Padawan Vernestra Rwoh.

PROTECTIVE SHIELD

During the Great Disaster, Stellan protects the people of Ta'klah from falling space debris. He leaps to the rescue from his flying Vector ship, shielding a child with the Force. Stellan then instructs the people of Ta'klah to run. He is promoted to the Jedi Council shortly after.

FAIR AND FOUL

Stellan helps organize the Jedi delegation to the Republic Fair on Valo, where he is assigned to protect Chancellor Lina Soh. At the Fair, Stellan comes up against former Jedi Ty Yorrick, who is employed by someone trying to sell a machine that can disrupt lightsabers. He confronts her and they duel, with Ty almost killing Stellan.

> "NO JEDI IS EVER ALONE. WE ARE UNITED IN THE FORCE."
>
> – Stellan Gios

Later, during the Nihil attack on the Fair, Stellan tries to get Soh and others to safety. He demonstrates his conviction that the Force should only be used defensively as he uses it to blow away the Nihil's poisonous war gas and to shield people without striking back.

LOYAL FRIEND

Stellan is open-minded and caring, happy to listen without judgment. When Elzar confides that he has touched the dark side, Stellan reassures his friend and suggests they take a meditation retreat to Jedha to ensure Elzar stays on the path of the light side.

NOBLE END

Stellan serves as temporary Marshal of Starlight Beacon, the symbol of the Republic's presence in the Outer Rim. When the station crashes toward the planet Eiram, Stellan remains on board to operate the navigation controls and guide it away from a busy city. Starlight crashes into the ocean, killing Stellan but saving thousands of lives on the ground.

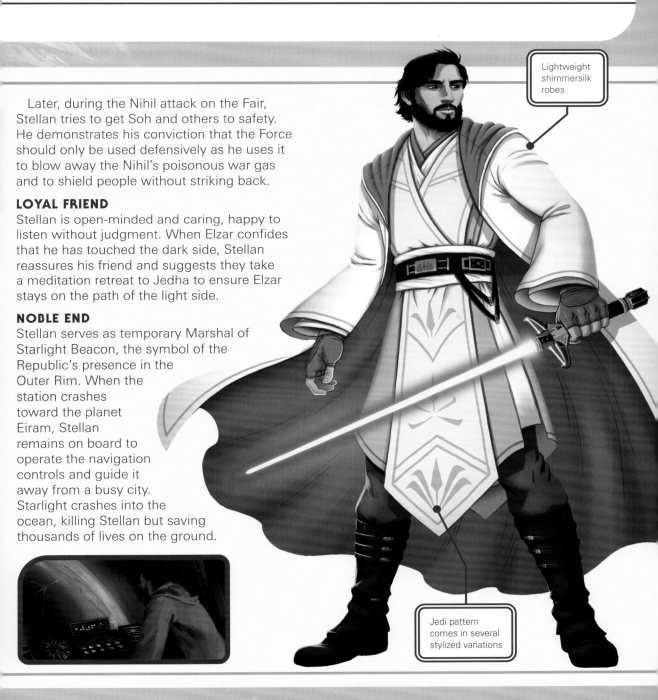

Lightweight shimmersilk robes

Jedi pattern comes in several stylized variations

AVAR KRISS

MARSHAL OF STARLIGHT BEACON

PRONOUNS: She/her
SPECIES: Human
HEIGHT: 1.73 m (5 ft 8 in)

ALLEGIANCE: Jedi Order
FIRST APPEARANCE: LotJ

Deeply loyal to the Jedi Order, Avar Kriss is one of the most powerful and respected Jedi Masters of her time. Raised and trained in the Coruscant Temple alongside her best friends, Stellan Gios and Elzar Mann, Avar soon rose through the ranks of the Order. All Jedi are encouraged to connect with the Force in their own way. Avar sees it as music and thinks of herself and her fellow Jedi as a great chorus. Others look up to her, and her guidance and empathy help shape the Order.

THE GREAT DISASTER

Avar's leadership skills save many lives after the ship *Legacy Run* tears apart in hyperspace and its plummeting debris puts the planets of the Hetzal system at risk. Avar coordinates a group of Jedi to help, connecting them all through the Force. She rescues refugees and prevents a cargo ship full of flammable tibanna gas from exploding.

This Great Disaster marks the first conflict between the Jedi and the Nihil, which eventually leads to a fierce rivalry between Avar and high-ranking Nihil Lourna Dee. It is also pivotal to Avar being named Marshal of Starlight Beacon, the Republic's Outer Rim space station, built as a symbol of hope, and to invite other star systems into the Republic.

CLASH WITH THE DRENGIR

In one of the first clashes between the Jedi and the carnivorous Drengir creatures, the brainwashed Jedi Master Sskeer captures Avar on the planet Sedri Minor. Avar narrowly escapes, along with fellow Jedi Keeve Trennis and Sskeer, who is no longer under Drengir control. The Hutts have a stake on Sedri Minor, and—in a rare moment of diplomacy—they agree to fight alongside Avar and the Jedi. They eventually chase the Drengir to their Great Progenitor, the being who links her root-mind to the others, and capture her for study.

LIGHT OF THE JEDI

Avar's compassionate and optimistic nature sometimes clashes with a sense of duty that pushes her to fight on, no matter the odds.

Jeweled diadem gifted by Stellan and Elzar

As marshal, Avar often wears formal gold robes

"THE SONG OF THE FORCE WILL LIFT US ALL."

– Avar Kriss

Her focus on pursuing Lourna Dee, whom she believes to be the leader of the Nihil, causes other Jedi to worry that Avar is too focused on a personal grudge. Later, Avar tries and fails to save fellow Jedi Estala Maru during the fall of Starlight Beacon, leaving her with deep guilt about losing the station and the people within.

ELZAR MANN

CHARMING MAVERICK

PRONOUNS: He/him
SPECIES: Human
HEIGHT: 1.80 m (5 ft 11 in)

ALLEGIANCE: Jedi Order
FIRST APPEARANCE: LotJ

Elzar Mann is a Jedi who constantly pushes boundaries. He sees the Force as a deep, dark ocean, and sometimes he's tempted to jump in. He often meditates in water, too. Elzar's focus on solving problems no matter the cost and his interest in experimenting with the Force make him a maverick within the Jedi Order. Despite his feelings of duty to the Order, Elzar struggles with finding balance in the Force and he sometimes

gives in to his emotions. Elzar reflects carefully on his actions, and is hard on himself when he makes mistakes. He travels a bumpy path, but Elzar is determined to find the right balance.

CRISIS TEAM
Elzar was trained by Jedi Master Roland Quarry and became close friends with Avar Kriss and Stellan Gios. As Padawans, Elzar and Avar become close, but honor the Jedi rule of nonattachment. Elzar, Avar, and Stellan fight side by side during the Great Disaster on Hetzal. Working together with Republic analyst Keven Tarr, Elzar and Avar save many lives by building a network of droid processors that calculates where dangerous debris is likely to emerge from hyperspace.

DARK CLOUDS OVERHEAD
When the Nihil attack the Republic Fair on Valo, Elzar taps into the dark side of the Force to throw the Fair's floating pavilions at the pirate fleet. Afterward, Elzar admits his failings to Stellan. Instead of criticizing, his friend is sympathetic and recommends that Elzar take some time to communicate with the Force on

> "TO KNOW THE DARKNESS IS TO BEGIN TO CONTROL IT."
>
> — Elzar Mann

the moon of Jedha. Elzar later trains with Jedi Wayseeker Orla Jareni. She helps him find balance with the Force by showing him that he should listen to the Force but not be overwhelmed by it.

STARLIGHT BEACON RESCUE

Elzar and Orla are on board the Starlight Beacon when the Nihil attack. They join Stellan in keeping people calm and evacuating as many as possible. Elzar coordinates a team of astromech droids to take the station apart from the inside, giving trapped civilian ships a way to escape. Calling on the Force more strongly than he has in a long time, Elzar opens the station's gigantic bay doors and tries to steer the crashing Starlight Beacon away from the planet Eiram.

During the rescue, Elzar kills ex-Nihil scientist Chancey Yarrow, thinking she is sabotaging the system, when really she is trying to repair the thrusters. Elzar later reunites with Avar. He must live with the guilt of knowing he killed Chancey when the scientist could have helped save the station.

Confident stance shows his determination

Formal gold robes with a Jedi pattern

Plain boots are a Jedi staple

LODEN GREATSTORM

WISE AND IMPOSING MASTER

Temple attire

Lightsaber was recovered by the Nihil and kept as a trophy by Marchion Ro after Loden's death

PRONOUNS: He/him
SPECIES: Twi'lek
HEIGHT: 1.96 m (6 ft 5 in)

ALLEGIANCE: Jedi Order
FIRST APPEARANCE: LotJ

One of the most respected Jedi Masters, Loden Greatstorm is highly skilled in combat, but he knows that the most powerful leaders can prevent violence before it starts. Loden has years of Jedi experience that enables him to make smart, informed decisions during moments of conflict. As Bell Zettifar's master, he pushes his student to embrace failure as a part of the learning process.

TRAGIC END

Brave, wise, and patient, Loden is admired by his fellow Jedi, which makes his kidnapping by the Nihil all the more unsettling. During his captivity, Loden finds the strength to connect back to the Force and briefly escapes, but he is killed by the Nameless creature known as the Leveler soon after.

"IF I DO EVERYTHING, NO ONE
LEARNS ANYTHING."

– **Loden Greatstorm**

SSKEER

GRUFF JEDI MASTER

Sskeer relies on his heightened senses as much as the Force when tracking enemies

Sskeer prefers to go barefoot

PRONOUNS: He/him
SPECIES: Trandoshan
HEIGHT: 1.68 m (5 ft 6 in)

ALLEGIANCE: Jedi Order
FIRST APPEARANCE: LotJ

Known as a strong, blunt Jedi Master, Sskeer is also a compassionate mentor. He is very proud of his Padawan, Keeve Trennis, and pushes her to believe in herself. Sskeer is diagnosed with Magrak syndrome, a rare disease that causes him to experience aggressive urges. The syndrome damages Sskeer's connection with the Force.

UNKNOWN FUTURE
Because Magrak syndrome has no cure, Avar Kriss wants to relieve Sskeer of his Jedi duties. Yet, during the fall of Starlight Beacon, Sskeer's weaker Force connection means the Nameless creatures do not affect him. This allows him to push them back while other Jedi evacuate the space station.

> "BEING A JEDI IS ABOUT CHOOSING THE LIGHT OVER AND OVER AGAIN."
> – Sskeer

VERNESTRA RWOH

TEEN JEDI PRODIGY

Lightsaber blade can change into a flexible whip

PRONOUNS: She/her
SPECIES: Mirialan
HEIGHT: 1.68 m (5 ft 6 in)

ALLEGIANCE: Jedi Order
FIRST APPEARANCE: AToC

Vernestra Rwoh's confidence and faith in the Force are the reasons she became, at age 15, one of the youngest Jedi Knights ever. Some of her abilities are a mystery even to herself. She feels an uncanny connection to hyperspace, often falling into confusing visions during faster-than-light jumps. Vernestra wields a purple-bladed lightsaber that transforms into a rare lightwhip.

FINDING A FRIEND

Despite her young age, Vernestra trains a Padawan of her own, Imri Cantaros. Sometimes, Vernestra's confidence can come off as dismissive, but she has a strong sense of empathy toward others. She likes to focus on her training and is not distracted by the idea of romance. In fact, she talks to Imri about her experiences as someone who is aromantic, which means she is not interested in romance with anyone.

"REVENGE IS NOT THE WAY OF THE LIGHT."

– Vernestra Rwoh

BELL ZETTIFAR

DETERMINED JEDI PADAWAN

Brown mission robes are sturdier than formal gold ones

PRONOUNS: He/him
SPECIES: Human
HEIGHT: 1.78 m (5 ft 10 in)
ALLEGIANCE: Jedi Order
FIRST APPEARANCE: LotJ

Bell Zettifar learns to believe in himself from his Jedi Master, Loden Greatstorm. Together they overcome challenges including fighting against the Nihil, and Bell learns to control his landing after falling from a great height. In one of his first missions as a Jedi, Bell clashes with the Nihil. The marauders unleash a monster, which later kills Loden.

A NEW MASTER

Master Indeera Stokes takes Bell under her wing as her new Padawan. Mourning Loden, Bell is on board Starlight Beacon when the space station is attacked. Along with the Jedi Burryaga, Bell helps civilians evacuate to safety. Burry goes missing as Starlight falls, but Bell never gives up on his fellow Padawan, and he continues to search for his friend.

CHARHOUND FRIEND

Ember the charhound's loyalty and ferocity help Bell as he goes along on his Jedi journey. Charhounds are known for their fire breath, and Ember is no exception—her mouth burns hot enough to melt metal.

Charhound fur tends to stick to clothing

"THESE ARE MY PEOPLE. IT'S MY JOB TO HELP THEM IF I CAN."

– Bell Zettifar

BURRYAGA

EMPATHETIC PADAWAN

Wooden hilt made from wroshyr trees on Kashyyyk

Thick fur protects against rough weather

PRONOUNS: He/him
SPECIES: Wookiee
HEIGHT: 2.24 m (7 ft 4 in)

ALLEGIANCE: Jedi Order
FIRST APPEARANCE: SS: GT

Burryaga, or Burry, is a kind, empathetic Jedi. During the Great Disaster, he is able to sense survivors that other Jedi cannot, which leads to their rescue. While he is always helpful, Burry can be shy, especially around those who don't speak his language. His Jedi Master, Nib Assek, teaches herself the Wookiee language, Shyriiwook, while she trains Burry, leading to a close friendship.

BRAVE IN BATTLE
Burry is aboard Starlight Beacon during the Nihil attack. He throws himself into battle against deadly rathtars, risking his life to save others. But as Starlight falls, Burry disappears. He ends up stranded in a deep-sea cavern on Eiram before making contact with Bell Zettifar.

"ALL LIFE IS PRECIOUS, AND WE ARE ALL THE REPUBLIC."

– Burryaga

TEREC AND CERET

JEDI BOND-TWINS

The twins regularly dress the same

Both twins wield green lightsabers

PRONOUNS: Both: They/them
SPECIES: Kotabi
HEIGHT: 1.73 m (5 ft 8 in)

ALLEGIANCE: Jedi Order
FIRST APPEARANCE: THR (PI)

Jedi Knights Terec and Ceret are Kotabi bond-twins, which means they share one mind and know each other's thoughts to a degree. When one twin is injured, the other is similarly affected, even when they are a great distance apart. They can also sense strong emotions in those around them. Both twins show patience when others struggle to tell them apart.

HURT AND HEALING
While the twins can feel each other's pain, they can also help each other heal. When Terec's undercover mission goes wrong and the Nameless attacks them, Ceret sends both twins into a hibernation state, which slows down Terec's body as it starts turning to stone.

"WE ARE, IN ESSENCE THE SAME BEING. AT THE LEAST, THE SAME MIND."

– Ceret

LULA TALISOLA

THOUGHTFUL PADAWAN

Hair braided with blue beads

Gauntlets protect wrists in close combat

PRONOUNS: She/her
SPECIES: Human
HEIGHT: 1.65 m (5 ft 5 in)

ALLEGIANCE: Jedi Order
FIRST APPEARANCE:
THRA (PI)

Lula Talisola's talents as a Padawan extend well beyond her abilities with a lightsaber. Her compassion leads her to welcome the young, Force-sensitive Zeen Mrala into her crew on the mobile Padawan training ship *Star Hopper*. Trained by Master Kantam Sy, Lula is close to many other Jedi, including Farzala Tarabal and Qort.

SEARCHING HER FEELINGS

Lula has spent her entire life dreaming of becoming a Jedi Knight, but when the day comes and Masters Torban Buck and Kantam Sy say she's ready, Lula hesitates. She chooses to take some time to focus on her newfound feelings for Zeen, and see whether that love means she has a future in the Jedi Order.

"I HAVE TO MAKE SENSE OF SOME THINGS... MY FEELINGS FOR HER."

– Lula Talisola

INDEERA STOKES

PRONOUNS: She/her
SPECIES: Tholothian
HEIGHT: 1.75 m (5 ft 9 in)

ALLEGIANCE: Jedi Order
FIRST APPEARANCE: LotJ

"DO NOT GLORY IN THE DEATH OF YOUR ENEMY. THAT WAY LEADS TO THE DARK SIDE."

– Indeera Stokes

Indeera Stokes is a Jedi Knight with a difficult task—taking over as Bell Zettifar's master after Loden Greatstorm is presumed dead. Known for her sharp sense of humor, Indeera is also very compassionate toward others. She tries to balance honoring Bell's grief over losing his former master with pushing him to continue with his studies as a Padawan. Indeera possesses unique levels of concentration, even for a Jedi. She displays this ability on a mission against the Nihil when she pilots two Vector starships at once—one physically and one remotely—using the Force.

Leather vambrace

Lightsaber holster

NIB ASSEK

PRONOUNS: She/her
SPECIES: Human
HEIGHT: 1.65 m (5 ft 5 in)

ALLEGIANCE: Jedi Order
FIRST APPEARANCE: SS: GT

"TOGETHER WE CAN DO ANYTHING THROUGH THE FORCE."

– Nib Assek

Nib Assek is a compassionate, caring Jedi Knight, which makes her an excellent match for the Wookiee Burryaga, a particularly empathetic Padawan. Nib takes her role as a teacher to heart, learning the tricky Wookiee language Shyriiwook so she can communicate fully with her Padawan. Nib's ability to understand her apprentice helps save lives during the Great Disaster. She is the only one to realize that Burry can sense survivors on a piece of debris, even though he is unable to communicate this to the others. She speaks up for Burry, and stops the squadron from shooting down the debris.

Lightsaber held in a reverse grip

IMRI CANTAROS

PRONOUNS: He/him
SPECIES: Human
HEIGHT: 1.78 m (5 ft 10 in)

ALLEGIANCE: Jedi Order
FIRST APPEARANCE: LotJ

Padawan Imri Cantaros has exceptional Force empathy. His sensitivity to others' feelings gives him great insight but can also be overwhelming. Imri's mentor, Master Douglas Sunvale, dies in a Nihil attack, and Imri's grief and anger lead him close to the dark side. He sets off to seek revenge against the Nihil on the jungle moon Wevo, but Vernestra Rwoh pulls him back. Despite their similar ages, she becomes his next master. The pair develop a deep bond over the course of their missions together.

> "I DON'T THINK I'M CUT OUT TO BE A JEDI."
>
> – Imri Cantaros

Lightsaber design inspired by Avar Kriss

New formal robes issued after Wevo crisis

KANTAM SY

PRONOUNS: They/them
SPECIES: Human
HEIGHT: 1.75 m (5 ft 9 in)

ALLEGIANCE: Jedi Order
FIRST APPEARANCE: THRA (PI)

Kantam Sy was Master Yoda's Padawan, and later master to Lula Talisola. Gentle and easygoing among friends, Kantam is a fierce fighter in battle against enemies. During the Great Disaster, Kantam is part of a team that helps evacuate the ship *Voyager Dawn*. They also fly a Vector starship during a conflict against the Nihil, saving the life of Jedi Torban Buck before emerging victorious. Kantam leads a mixed group of Jedi and Corellian citizens, including Svi'no Atchapat in battle against the Nihil, who are attempting to take over the Coronet City shipyards.

> "WE COME IN PEACE."
>
> – Kantam Sy

ORLA JARENI

PRONOUNS: She/her
SPECIES: Umbaran
HEIGHT: 1.70 m (5 ft 7 in)

ALLEGIANCE: Jedi Order
FIRST APPEARANCE: ItD

As a Wayseeker, Orla Jareni goes where the Force leads her, operating separately from the Jedi Council. Orla is witty and fiercely independent, but works well with other Jedi when she feels the Force has called her to a mission or cause. Her unique perspectives about the Jedi and the Force make her an excellent mentor to Jedi Elzar Mann when he finds himself drawing on the dark side of the Force. Like her ideas about the Force, Orla's lightsaber is unusual—white, double-bladed, and with a hinge at its midpoint.

"MY PRAISE IS DIFFICULT TO EARN. THAT'S WHY IT'S WORTH SOMETHING TO YOU, I HOPE."

– Orla Jareni

OBRATUK GLII

PRONOUNS: He/him
SPECIES: Parwan
HEIGHT: 2.24 m (7 ft 4 in)

ALLEGIANCE: Jedi Order
FIRST APPEARANCE: THRA (PI)

Skilled swordfighter Obratuk Glii is Farzala Tarabal's Jedi Master. Parwans live long lives, so Glii has trained—and outlived—many Padawans. He travels with the crew of the *Vessel* to a diplomatic meeting with the Hutts. Later, during the fall of Starlight Beacon, he is captured by Nihil leader Marchion Ro. Aboard the *Gaze Electric*, Ro sets a Nameless upon Glii, ending his life.

"I AM A JEDI. THE FORCE IS MY ALLY. I HAVE NOTHING TO FEAR."

– Obratuk Glii

Parwans can make themselves float by filling themselves with gasses

One of four tendrils that function similarly to additional limbs

FARZALA TARABAL

PRONOUNS: He/him
SPECIES: Zygerrian
HEIGHT: 1.70 m (5 ft 7 in)

ALLEGIANCE: Jedi Order
FIRST APPEARANCE:
THRA (PI)

Farzala Tarabal is a Padawan with a mischievous sense of humor. He is close friends with fellow Padawans Qort and Lula Talisola on the mobile Jedi academy *Star Hopper*. Trained by Master Obratuk Glii, Farzala shows talent in both lightsaber combat and diplomacy. He uses Master Obratuk's teachings about fear to help escape captivity when a peace negotiation on the planet Nal Hutta goes wrong. Farzala's missions see him battle the Nihil and the Drengir across the galaxy before he is knighted alongside his friend Qort.

"THE JEDI BECOMES A MASTER BY FACING OUR FEAR, NOT PRETENDING WE DON'T FEEL IT."

– Farzala Tarabal

QORT

PRONOUNS: He/him
SPECIES: Aloxian
HEIGHT: 1.22 m (4 ft)
ALLEGIANCE: Jedi Order

FIRST APPEARANCE:
THRA (PI)

Qort is a Padawan who trains under Master Tabakan Pak on the *Star Hopper*. As an Aloxian, Qort was born with naturally destructive tendencies. Wearing a vonduun crab skull mask since he was an infant has helped balance his emotions. Qort is known for being kind, and he is a good friend to fellow Padawans Farzala Tarabal and Lula Talisola. Qort's work for the Jedi Order takes him to Takodana—where his Force sensitivity was first discovered years earlier—to help defend it from the Nihil. His mask breaks during the mission, but he and his friends quickly embrace his new look and go on to defeat the Nihil.

"I AM READY."

– Qort

Vonduun crab skull mask worn until maturity

Blue sash matches lightsaber

LILY TORA-ASI

PROBLEM-SOLVING JEDI

Lily's two lightsabers are identical

High boots protect legs during combat

PRONOUNS: She/her
SPECIES: Human
HEIGHT: 1.65 m (5 ft 5 in)

ALLEGIANCE: Jedi Order
FIRST APPEARANCE:
TEoB, V1

Lily Tora-Asi is a Jedi Knight stationed at the outpost on the planet Banchii. With her Padawan, Keerin Fionn, Lily takes her role as protector of the refugees settling on Banchii seriously. However, she regularly questions her own decisions. Over time, she learns to rely on her instincts to find unique solutions to the problems she faces on her Jedi journey.

DRENGIR DEFEAT

Lily is skilled in Jar'Kai lightsaber combat, which focuses on using two lightsabers at once. But when she discovers that lightsabers are useless against the Drengir, Lily has another idea. She lures the Drengir to a lake where she and the other Jedi create a water whirlwind to destroy them.

> "DUELING IS MORE THAN JUST WIELDING A WEAPON. YOU MUST TRUST YOUR INTENTION TO WIN."
>
> – Lily Tora-Asi

ARKOFF

STERN JEDI TEACHER

Jedi robes modified for Wookiee comfort

Belt holds emergency rescue and medical tools

PRONOUNS: He/him
SPECIES: Wookiee
HEIGHT: 2.49 m (8 ft 2 in)

ALLEGIANCE: Jedi Order
FIRST APPEARANCE: TEoB, V1

Arkoff was trained by Master Ravna Abronsa, and he fights alongside her and his former Padawan, Azlin Rell, at the Battle of Dalna. Arkoff visits Rell several times afterward, and later hides Rell's journal, which contains the secrets of the Nameless. As a master, Arkoff instructs Lily Tora-Asi, her Padawan Keerin Fionn, and younglings Nima Allets and Viv'Nia Nia'Viv at the Banchii outpost. He encourages his students to be open-minded.

LEADING BY EXAMPLE

Master Arkoff is a strict but effective teacher. His students look to him in times of danger, such as when a mysterious disturbance in the woods is discovered to be the deadly, plantlike Drengir. Arkoff opens the Jedi outpost to villagers fleeing the attack before heading off, with his fellow Jedi, to fight the monsters.

"THERE'S A LOT I NEED TO DISCUSS WITH MASTER ARKOFF."

– Lily Tora-Asi

REATH SILAS

ASPIRING ARCHIVIST

Padawan braids are an ancient Jedi tradition

PRONOUNS: He/him
SPECIES: Human
HEIGHT: 1.73 m (5 ft 8 in)

ALLEGIANCE: Jedi Order
FIRST APPEARANCE: ItD

Reath Silas' hard work and love of knowledge make him a skilled Padawan, but he prefers the library to the battlefield. He was close to his master, Jora Malli, before her death in a Nihil attack. Jedi Master Cohmac Vitus, who enjoys research just as much as Reath does, steps in as Reath's new master.

EXPANDING HIS HORIZONS

Reath and his allies, including *Vessel* pilot Affie Hollow, discover the Amaxine space station, which is infested with Drengir. Knowing he must rely on more than ancient texts to stay alive, Reath holds his own against the

monsters and resists the pull of dark-side artifacts, all the while grappling with his feelings for Nan, a member of the Nihil.

"HOW CAN WE STUDY THE DEEPEST SECRETS OF THE FORCE... IF WE'RE TOO BUSY FIGHTING TO STAY ALIVE?"

– Reath Silas

RAM JOMARAM

PADAWAN MECHANIC

Goggles keep eyes safe from errant sparks

Bonbrak mechanic

Ram's elderly droid, V-18, is sometimes mistaken for a rusty crate, though it has been upgraded with a repulsorlift and various weapons

PRONOUNS: He/him
SPECIES: Human
HEIGHT: 1.68 m (5 ft 6 in)

ALLEGIANCE: Jedi Order
FIRST APPEARANCE: RtCT

Ram Jomaram is a friendly, optimistic teen, most at home in a greasy, cluttered garage workshop. He becomes a Padawan at the Valo Jedi temple under Master Vasivola. Ram struggles with lightsaber combat but finds building and repairing vehicles and droids natural and meditative. In turn, it strengthens his connection to the Force.

GOOD COMMUNICATION

Ram teams up with Jedi Lula Talisola, her friend Zeen Mrala, and monster hunter Ty Yorrick when the Nihil attack. Their path to a downed communications tower is blocked by the Drengir, so Ram persuades the creatures to attack the Nihil instead of the Jedi. Ram and his local pit crew, the Bonbraks, repair the comms tower, and Ram decides to travel with his new friends to see the galaxy.

"I MIGHT STILL BE ABLE TO FIX IT."

– Ram Jomaram

ESTALA MARU

STARLIGHT BEACON HEAD OF OPERATIONS

Quick to process many details at once

Often levitates through the Force when truly focused

PRONOUNS: He/him
SPECIES: Kessurian
HEIGHT: 1.88 m (6 ft 2 in)

ALLEGIANCE: Jedi Order
FIRST APPEARANCE: THR (PI)

Estala Maru is the Jedi Master in charge of operations at Starlight Beacon—the Republic's space station in the Outer Rim. Every day is different for Estala as he juggles the needs of Republic officials, Jedi Knights, and visitors to Starlight, while keeping track of every small detail. Estala's surprisingly sarcastic sense of humor endears him to his fellow Jedi.

SENSE OF DUTY
Estala is regularly pulled in different directions while doing his job, despite the help of his astromech droid, KC-78. But the safety of those on board Starlight Beacon is his highest priority. When an enormous explosion rips Starlight apart, Estala calls upon the Force to hold it together for as long as he can, sacrificing his own life to give others more time to evacuate.

"STARLIGHT IS UNDER ATTACK."

– Estala Maru

TORBAN BUCK

JEDI HEALER

Thick head tentacles

Belted tunic worn over robes

PRONOUNS: He/him
SPECIES: Chagrian
HEIGHT: 2.03 m (6 ft 8 in)

ALLEGIANCE: Jedi Order
FIRST APPEARANCE: THRA (PI)

Master Torban Buck is a Jedi healer with the strangely ominous nickname "Buckets of Blood." Buck is skilled in combat but, despite his nickname, avoids violence if possible. He is stationed on the *Star Hopper* with Jedi Master Yoda, overseeing a group of Padawans. Buck enjoys telling over-the-top, gory stories to the delight of Padawans and younglings, but he also has the rare ability to bring calm to chaotic situations.

GALACTIC BAKE-OFF

Torban Buck takes his role as a teacher and mentor seriously. He cares a lot for his students, and he shows it. Buck knows the importance of letting the young Jedi have fun, as he proves by hosting bake-off competitions and other entertaining contests, races, and activities.

"BUCKETS OF BLOOD HAS ARRIVED ON THE SCENE!"

– Torban Buck

COHMAC VITUS

JEDI SCHOLAR

Belt pouches hold survival supplies

PRONOUNS: He/him
SPECIES: Human
HEIGHT: 1.80 m (5 ft 11 in)

ALLEGIANCE: Jedi Order (formerly)
FIRST APPEARANCE: ItD

Cohmac Vitus sees himself as rational and logical, though he later develops a fascination with folklore and mysticism. His best friend is Jedi Orla Jareni, and they go through a lot together, including witnessing the death of Cohmac's master, Simmix. Unlike Orla, Cohmac tends to focus on his anger, and this often distresses him.

KILLING BLOW ON CORELLIA
Cohmac and fellow Jedi Master Kantam Sy investigate a Nihil plot on the planet Corellia. Cohmac feels conflicted about staying there instead of defending Starlight Beacon, which is under attack. When he senses Orla die on the crashing space station, the trauma of all the recent events leads him to leave the Order.

"IF WE STAY, WE STAY AND FIGHT."

– Cohmac Vitus

EMERICK CAPHTOR

JEDI INVESTIGATOR

Q-2 droid assists Emerick with his investigations

Vambraces offer added protection

Weatherproof greaves cover boots

PRONOUNS: He/him
SPECIES: Human
HEIGHT: 1.80 m (5 ft 11 in)

ALLEGIANCE: Jedi Order
FIRST APPEARANCE: OotS

Jedi Master Emerick Caphtor was tasked with investigating the death of Loden Greatstorm during the Battle of Grizal. Emerick has a serious nature, and likes to reserve judgment until he has all the facts. While Emerick is at first unhappy about teaming up with private investigator Sian Holt, they grow close to one another as Emerick opens up to his partner.

RHYME OF THE NAMELESS
The key to the mystery of what happened to Loden Greatstorm lies in an old Jedi nursery rhyme that has haunted Emerick and fellow Jedi Stellan Gios since they were children. The rhyme tells of Shrii-Ka-Rai, also known as Eaters of the Force. Emerick discovers that these are the Nameless—creatures that feed on Force users and turn their bodies to dust.

"SOMETIMES I KNOW WHAT I'M DOING. NOW LET'S GO."
— Emerick Caphtor

PRA-TRE VETER

PRONOUNS: He/him
SPECIES: Tarnab
HEIGHT: 1.70 m (5 ft 7 in)

ALLEGIANCE: Jedi Order
FIRST APPEARANCE: THR (PI)

Pra-Tre Veter is one of the Jedi Council Grand Masters, who oversee many key decisions about the direction of the Jedi Order, including Avar Kriss' appointment to Marshal of Starlight Beacon. Pra-Tre and several fellow Council masters decide to call members of the Order back to Starlight Beacon when the Nihil attack. Veter is captured by the Nihil and held captive. He is killed by the Nameless on the one-year anniversary of the fall of Starlight Beacon.

Cane made from native tarn trees

Robes embroidered with Republic patterns

LAHRU

Crested head changes color according to mood

Custom cloak clasp added to formal robes

PRONOUNS: He/him
SPECIES: Anx
HEIGHT: 3.96 m (13 ft)

ALLEGIANCE: Jedi Order
FIRST APPEARANCE: LotJ

Lahru is another Jedi Council Grand Master. He is known as one the wisest and most powerful Jedi, and is trusted with making important decisions about the future of the Order. Lahru is on board Starlight Beacon to name Avar Kriss the marshal of the space station. He urges caution about bringing a Drengir-infected Hutt body onto Starlight, worried it may prove dangerous for all on board—fears that turn out to be well founded.

EPHRU SHINN

PRONOUNS: She/her
SPECIES: Mon Calamari
HEIGHT: 1.78 m (5 ft 10 in)

ALLEGIANCE: Jedi Order
FIRST APPEARANCE: LotJ

Master Ephru Shinn holds Yoda's seat on the Jedi Council while the legendary master is away. She firmly believes that the Jedi should be keepers of the peace, not warriors. When the Council first debates whether to join the Republic's fight against the Nihil, Ephru rejects the idea. Despite what the Jedi may have done in the past, she urges the Council to focus on their role in the present. She reasons that the Council has a chance to teach the Republic to embrace peace, but Grand Master Lahru and Master Yarael Poof argue against her.

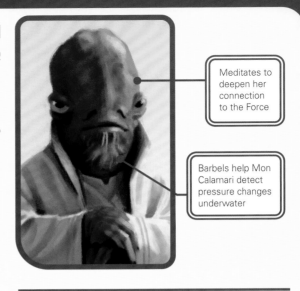

Meditates to deepen her connection to the Force

Barbels help Mon Calamari detect pressure changes underwater

"WHAT IS OUR ROLE IN THE REPUBLIC, AT THIS PRECISE MOMENT?"

– Ephru Shinn

JORA MALLI

PRONOUNS: She/her
SPECIES: Togruta
HEIGHT: 1.75 m (5 ft 9 in)

ALLEGIANCE: Jedi Order
FIRST APPEARANCE: LotJ

Jora Malli is a respected Jedi and Council member, though she also has a reputation for being more impulsive than thoughtful. She believes that whatever choice a Jedi makes is the will of the Force. Her light-side influence is powerful enough to heal corrupted artifacts. Jora trains two Padawans, Dez Rydan and Reath Silas. She plans to step down from the Council to become marshal on the Starlight Beacon space station. However, before she can take on her new role, her Vector fighter ship is attacked by the Nihil, and Jora perishes.

Headdress passed down from her Jedi Master

Ceremonial ornament holds head-tails in place

"WHATEVER THE FORCE WILLS."

– Jora Malli

RANA KANT

PRONOUNS: She/her
SPECIES: Duros
HEIGHT: 1.70 m (5 ft 7 in)

ALLEGIANCE: Jedi Order
FIRST APPEARANCE: LotJ

Rana Kant sits on the Jedi Council when it considers the critical question of whether the Jedi should pursue the Nihil on behalf of the Republic. Rana argues that while the Jedi have battle experience, they are not currently at war. Rana's former Padawan, Stellan Gios, takes her place on the Jedi Council after she dies of natural causes.

YARAEL POOF

PRONOUNS: He/him
SPECIES: Quermian
HEIGHT: 2.64 m (8 ft 8 in)

ALLEGIANCE: Jedi Order
FIRST APPEARANCE: LotJ

Yarael Poof is a powerful Jedi Master who specializes in mind touches and illusions. He works with Republic Chancellor Lina Soh to determine the cause of the Great Disaster, and he encourages the Jedi Council to join the Republic in its conflict with the Nihil. He is one of the Jedi that attends the opening ceremony for the space station Starlight Beacon.

TERI ROSASON

PRONOUNS: She/her
SPECIES: Human
HEIGHT: 1.60 m (5 ft 3 in)

ALLEGIANCE: Jedi Order
FIRST APPEARANCE: ItD

Teri Rosason is one of the Jedi Council members who review Cohmac Vitus, Reath Silas, and Orla Jareni's unsanctioned actions at the Amaxine station. Teri is sympathetic toward Reath and offers him some constructive advice for the future. Teri also criticizes Avar Kriss' alliance with the Hutts and encourages the Council to search for the Nihil leader.

RY KI-SAKKA

PRONOUNS: He/him
SPECIES: Human
HEIGHT: 1.88 m (6 ft 2 in)

ALLEGIANCE: Jedi Order
FIRST APPEARANCE: THRS

Ry Ki-Sakka steps up to take Jora Malli's place on the Jedi Council after her death at the Battle of Kur. Ry has spent most of his time as a Jedi on missions in remote parts of the galaxy. He brings his past experiences to his role on the Council, where, as a Grand Master, he exemplifies what the Jedi stand for.

OPPO RANCISIS

PRONOUNS: He/him
SPECIES: Thisspiasian
HEIGHT: 1.35 m (4 ft 5 in)

ALLEGIANCE: Jedi Order
FIRST APPEARANCE: LotJ

Oppo Rancisis is a highly respected member of the Jedi Council. He rescues a young Lourna Dee from Zygerrian criminals and mentors her, hoping to help her live a disciplined life. As a Thisspiasian, Oppo has a very long life span. His many years of service and vast experience give him a unique perspective when offering advice to the Council.

KEATON MURAG

PRONOUNS: He/him
SPECIES: Human
HEIGHT: 1.83 m (6 ft)

ALLEGIANCE: Jedi Order
FIRST APPEARANCE: LotJ

Jedi Master Keaton Murag is appointed to the Jedi Council just before the Great Disaster. He is present for the pivotal meeting where the Council votes to join the Republic and fight against the Nihil. Keaton works hard to find ways of keeping the Council up to date with galactic goings on.

ADAMPO

PRONOUNS: He/him
SPECIES: Yarkoran
HEIGHT: 1.98 m (6 ft 6 in)

ALLEGIANCE: Jedi Order
FIRST APPEARANCE: LotJ

Council Master Adampo believes Jedi are not meant to be warriors. He opposes the Council taking military action against the Nihil after the Great Disaster, but his side loses the vote by one.

"THE JEDI ARE NOT A MILITARY FORCE."

– Adampo

ADA-LI CARRO

PRONOUNS: She/her
SPECIES: Human
HEIGHT: 1.63 m (5 ft 4 in)

ALLEGIANCE: Jedi Order
FIRST APPEARANCE: LotJ

Ada-Li Carro sits on the Jedi Council alongside Yoda, Oppo Rancisis, and nine other masters during the time of the Great Disaster. She brings decades of experience and wisdom to her role on the Council, and her advice is appreciated by the other members.

SOLEIL AGRA

PRONOUNS: She/her
SPECIES: Nautolan
HEIGHT: 1.75 m (5 ft 9 in)
ALLEGIANCE: Jedi Order
FIRST APPEARANCE: TEoB, V2

After the fall of Starlight Beacon, Jedi Master Soleil Agra is one of the Jedi who transmits a message across the galaxy—that all Jedi should regroup on the planet Coruscant as soon as possible. Like all Nautolans, Agra can use her head-tails to sense how others are feeling, an ability that serves her well in her role on the Jedi Council.

NYLA QUINN

PRONOUNS: She/her
SPECIES: Twi'lek
HEIGHT: 1.63 m (5 ft 4 in)
ALLEGIANCE: Jedi Order
FIRST APPEARANCE: MtD

Nyla Quinn is the friendly master of the Dalna Jedi temple. Along with her fellow Dalna Jedi, Lyssa Votz and Yacek Sparkburn, Nyla welcomes Vernestra Rwoh and Imri Cantaros during their search for the kidnapped Avon Starros. With them, Nyla helps free a group of children captured by the Nihil.

LYSSA VOTZ

PRONOUNS: She/her
SPECIES: Human
HEIGHT: 1.65 m (5 ft 5 in)
ALLEGIANCE: Jedi Order
FIRST APPEARANCE: MtD

Lyssa Votz is the archivist at Dalna's small Jedi temple. She is reluctant to use violence, but when she finds herself in danger with fellow Jedi Vernestra Rwoh, Lyssa drives away a pack of ice gators.

"I LOVE THIS
LITTLE PLANET."

– Lyssa Votz

YACEK SPARKBURN

PRONOUNS: He/him
SPECIES: Human
HEIGHT: 1.88 m (6 ft 2 in)
ALLEGIANCE: Jedi Order
FIRST APPEARANCE: MtD

Yacek Sparkburn enjoys meeting new people and cooking delicious meals. He vastly prefers either of those pastimes to meditation or dueling. Yacek helps Vernestra Rwoh and Imri Cantaros rescue Avon Starros from the Nihil.

KEERIN FIONN

PRONOUNS: He/him
SPECIES: Human
HEIGHT: 1.68 m (5 ft 6 in)
ALLEGIANCE: Jedi Order

FIRST APPEARANCE:
TEoB, V1

Padawan Keerin Fionn spars with his master, Lily Tora-Asi, to help teach the younglings at the Jedi outpost on Banchii. Thoughtful and kind, Keerin can also be impulsive and reckless. The Nihil take advantage of his rush to help a local settler, with devastating results.

RUUSSTHA VIDYARVRIKT

PRONOUNS: She/her
SPECIES: Ongree
HEIGHT: 1.65 m (5 ft 5 in)

ALLEGIANCE: Jedi Order
FIRST APPEARANCE:
THR: ToS

Ruusstha Vidyarvrikt is a nursemaid on Dalna. She sings a nursery rhyme to the younglings in her care, Emerick Caphtor and Stellan Gios. At the time, the song scares the children, but when Emerick later becomes a Jedi Knight he realizes it holds the key to learning more about the Nameless.

NOORANBAKARAKANA

PRONOUNS: She/her
SPECIES: Frozian
HEIGHT: 1.75 m (5 ft 9 in)

ALLEGIANCE: Jedi Order
FIRST APPEARANCE: TRS

Nooranbakarakana, or Nooran for short, is a calm and deliberate Jedi Knight. She is well-known within the Jedi Order for being able to keep her mind clear so she can focus on solving problems, even during the chaos of battle or galactic emergencies.

ORBALIN

PRONOUNS: He/him
SPECIES: Ugor
HEIGHT: 1.70 m (5 ft 7 in)

ALLEGIANCE: Jedi Order
FIRST APPEARANCE:
THR (PI)

OrbaLin is the Jedi archivist stationed on board Starlight Beacon. The first Ugor to ever become a Jedi, OrbaLin wears a space suit to contain his green, shapeless body. While some find OrbaLin's lectures boring, he plays an important role in discovering the threat of the Drengir on Starlight Beacon and calling for help when the Nihil attack the Republic Fair.

VIV'NIA NIA'VIV

PRONOUNS: She/her
SPECIES: Togruta
HEIGHT: 1.25 m (4 ft 1 in)

ALLEGIANCE: Jedi Order
FIRST APPEARANCE:
TEoB, V1

A youngling at the Banchii Jedi outpost, Viv'Nia Nia'Viv works hard to control the Force, though she can struggle to focus her thoughts. Viv is filled with a desire to help those around her, though she wishes she didn't live in such a remote place.

NIMA ALLETS

PRONOUNS: She/her
SPECIES: Human
HEIGHT: 1.37 m (4 ft 6 in)

ALLEGIANCE: Jedi Order
FIRST APPEARANCE:
TEoB, V1

Nima Allets and her friend, Viv'Nia Nia'Viv, are younglings at the Jedi outpost on Banchii. Nima is thoughtful and inquisitive, and enjoys spending time with other Jedi during a visit to Starlight Beacon. Nima is also a talented artist who makes Viv a new headpiece.

LYNELA KABE-OYU

PRONOUNS: She/her
SPECIES: Kel Dor
HEIGHT: 1.75 m (5 ft 9 in)

ALLEGIANCE: Jedi Order
FIRST APPEARANCE:
THRA: A

Master Lynela Kabe-Oyu is stationed at the Hynestia Prime Jedi outpost with Stellan Gios and his new Padawan, Vernestra Rwoh. Impressed with Vernestra's sparring skills, Kabe-Oyu invites her to a banquet. When trouble breaks out between the Hutts and Hynestians, Kabe-Oyu rescues the Hynestian royal family.

RU-RU

PRONOUNS: She/her
SPECIES: Imroosian
HEIGHT: Unknown

ALLEGIANCE: Jedi Order
FIRST APPEARANCE:
TEoB, V1

Kindhearted Ru-Ru is the archivist at the Jedi outpost on Banchii. In addition to helping fellow Jedi find information, she grows close to the civilians on the planet. Ru-Ru helps fight off the Drengir and evacuate settlers when the Nihil invade Banchii.

MIKKEL SUTMANI

PRONOUNS: He/him
SPECIES: Ithorian
HEIGHT: 1.90 m (6 ft 3 in)
ALLEGIANCE: Jedi Order
FIRST APPEARANCE: SS: GT

Master Mikkel Sutmani is one of several Jedi pilots who rescue passengers stranded in a cargo vessel during the Great Disaster. Mikkel is later killed by a Nihil while he pilots his Longbeam during the attack on the Republic Fair on Valo.

DAL AZIM

PRONOUNS: He/him
SPECIES: Human
HEIGHT: 1.68 m (5 ft 6 in)
ALLEGIANCE: Jedi Order
FIRST APPEARANCE: TR

Padawan Dal Azim and his Jedi Master, Oppo Rancisis, find themselves facing a group of Zygerrian criminals on one of their missions. Dal uses the Force to unlock the collar that sits around the neck of a teenage prisoner whose name is Lourna Dee.

"IT'S GOING TO BE ALL RIGHT NOW."

– Dal Azim to Lourna Dee

TE'AMI

PRONOUNS: She/her
SPECIES: Duros
HEIGHT: 1.73 m (5 ft 8 in)
ALLEGIANCE: Jedi Order
FIRST APPEARANCE: SS: GT

Te'Ami is a Jedi pilot sent out as part of a Longbeam squad during the Great Disaster. She teases fellow pilot Mikkel Sutmani about his friendliness toward her, but agrees to go on more missions with him. Before she gets the chance, though, her starfighter is shot down by a missile from Lourna Dee's ship.

GRISWAL

PRONOUNS: She/her
SPECIES: Unknown
HEIGHT: 71 cm (2 ft 4 in)
ALLEGIANCE: Jedi Order
FIRST APPEARANCE: THRA: TGBOS

Elderly Jedi Master Griswal is on board the *Voyager Dawn*, taking part in a meditation retreat for Jedi, when the Great Disaster strikes. She hides in the cruiser's garden, too afraid of the debris striking the ship to evacuate. But with Master Kantam Sy's help, Griswal fights her way out of the damaged ship, deflecting falling wreckage with her lightsaber.

DEZ RYDAN

PRONOUNS: He/him
SPECIES: Human
HEIGHT: 1.75 m (5 ft 9 in)

ALLEGIANCE: Jedi Order
FIRST APPEARANCE: ItD

Charming, skilled Dez Rydan is captured by the Drengir, brainwashed, and forced to fight fellow Padawan Reath Silas. Reath rescues him, but Dez feels he was influenced too  much by the Drengir and that his connection to the Force is damaged. He takes the Barash Vow, committing to years of meditation.

DOUGLAS SUNVALE

PRONOUNS: He/him
SPECIES: Human
HEIGHT: 1.83 m (6 ft)

ALLEGIANCE: Jedi Order
FIRST APPEARANCE: AToC

Jedi Master Douglas Sunvale is the marshal of the Jedi outpost on the Outer Rim planet Haileap. He and a group of young Jedi—including his own Padawan, Imri Cantaros—accompany the Dalnan diplomatic delegation to Starlight Beacon, but their ship is sabotaged by the Nihil. Douglas sacrifices himself to help Imri and the others reach an escape pod.

"THERE IS NOTHING TO FEAR."

– Douglas Sunvale

KLIAS TERADINE

PRONOUNS: He/him
SPECIES: Zeltron
HEIGHT: 1.73 m (5 ft 8 in)

ALLEGIANCE: Jedi Order
FIRST APPEARANCE: TRS

Curious Padawan Klias Teradine trains alongside Ty Yorrick with Master Cibaba at the Alaris Prime temple. He leads Ty into an abandoned shrine of the Yellow cult, seeking to understand the dark side in order to fight it. However, Klias becomes possessed by dark-side spirits and Ty is forced to kill him in the ensuing struggle.

CIBABA

PRONOUNS: He/him
SPECIES: Azumel
HEIGHT: 1.75 m (5 ft 9 in)

ALLEGIANCE: Jedi Order
FIRST APPEARANCE: TRS

Jedi Master Cibaba trains Padawan Klias Teradine and future monster hunter Ty Yorrick at the Jedi temple on Alaris Prime. He trains Ty to bond with animals, a skill that serves her well later in life, even though she is no longer a Jedi.

TABAKAN PAK

PRONOUNS: He/him
SPECIES: Dug
HEIGHT: 1.09 m (3 ft 7 in)
ALLEGIANCE: Jedi Order

FIRST APPEARANCE: THRA (PI)

Master Tabakan Pak copilots the Jedi training ship *Star Hopper* alongside Master Obratuk Glii. He's one of the Jedi who promote Qort and Farzala Tarabal from Padawans to Jedi Knights following their successful training on board *Star Hopper*.

REGALD COLL

PRONOUNS: He/him
SPECIES: Human
HEIGHT: 1.70 m (5 ft 7 in)
ALLEGIANCE: Jedi Order

FIRST APPEARANCE: TFS

Jedi Knight Regald Coll jokes around—even with the enemy. He oversees Nihil prisoners Nan and Chancey Yarrow, and his sense of humor shines through even under pressure. When the Nihil attack Starlight Beacon, Regald falls victim to the Nameless. But there's nothing amusing about his predicament, and a Nameless ends his life.

LARET SOVERAL

PRONOUNS: She/her
SPECIES: Human
HEIGHT: 1.68 m (5 ft 6 in)
ALLEGIANCE: Jedi Order

FIRST APPEARANCE: ItD

Master Laret Soveral mentors Orla Jareni in her Jedi training. The two sometimes clash, particularly when Laret gets frustrated by Orla's many questions. However, Laret is known for being tactful, and she makes sure to give her Padawan space. Laret accompanies Orla and fellow Jedi Cohmac Vitus on their mission to rescue the leaders of warring planets Eiram and E'ronoh.

"TO BE A JEDI IS TO SERVE."

– Laret Soveral

BIBS

PRONOUNS: He/him
SPECIES: Bravaisian
HEIGHT: 1.52 m (5 ft)
ALLEGIANCE: Jedi Order

FIRST APPEARANCE: THRA (PI)

Padawan Bibs studies the ways of the Jedi on the mobile training ship *Star Hopper*. He learns from Yoda, Torban Buck, and Lula Talisola. Bibs puts his Jedi training into practice when he investigates a distress signal on the planet Dol'har Hyde and locates Krix Kamerat's Nihil hideout.

MIRRO LOX

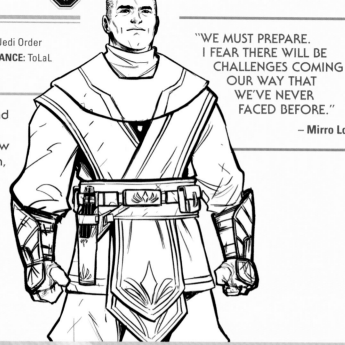

PRONOUNS: He/him
SPECIES: Human
HEIGHT: 1.83 m (6 ft)

ALLEGIANCE: Jedi Order
FIRST APPEARANCE: ToLaL

"WE MUST PREPARE.
I FEAR THERE WILL BE
CHALLENGES COMING
OUR WAY THAT
WE'VE NEVER
FACED BEFORE."

– Mirro Lox

Jedi Master Mirro Lox is a noble and charismatic leader who trained at the Jedi Temple on Coruscant a few years before Avar Kriss, Elzar Mann, and Stellan Gios. Mirro and his young Padawan, Amadeo Azzazzo, have been away on a long-term mission, so they were not involved in the Jedi Order's recent clashes with the Nihil. However, when the Council recalls all members of the Order to Coruscant, Miro volunteers himself and Amadeo to help.

AMADEO AZZAZZO

PRONOUNS: He/him
SPECIES: Human
HEIGHT: 1.73 m (5 ft 8 in)

ALLEGIANCE: Jedi Order
FIRST APPEARANCE: ToLaL

Amadeo Azzazzo is a Padawan apprenticed to Jedi Master Mirro Lox. Always ready for adventure, Amadeo is hungry for knowledge and wants to learn more about other cultures. After all the Jedi are recalled to Coruscant, Amadeo and his master are tasked with a new mission, aiding in the fight against the Nihil and the Nameless—foes that Amadeo has not encountered before.

"THE FORCE IS MY ANCHOR."

– Amadeo Azzazzo

GAVI

PRONOUNS: He/him
SPECIES: Human
HEIGHT: 1.57 m (5 ft 2 in)

ALLEGIANCE: Jedi Order
FIRST APPEARANCE: EfV

Jedi youngling Gavi is one of the best students in his class at the Jedi outpost on Valo. When the Nihil attack the planet, he witnesses the death of his Jedi Master at the hands of a Nameless. This event shakes his connection to the Force and causes the once confident Gavi to become anxious and fearful. After escaping and hiding out in the mountains, Gavi and his friends Tep Tep and Kildo move to the ruins of the Lonisa City Zoo, which was once a part of the Republic Fair.

TEP TEP

PRONOUNS: She/her
SPECIES: Alcedian
HEIGHT: 1.50 m (4 ft 11 in)

ALLEGIANCE: Jedi Order
FIRST APPEARANCE: EfV

Along with her friends Kildo and Gavi, Tep Tep is a Jedi youngling hiding from the Nihil on Valo. The trio live in the destroyed grounds of the Republic Fair, a space they share with a range of creatures who have escaped from the zoo. Tep Tep isn't scared by the ferocious neighbors—which include acklays, rathtars, sanvals, and hragscythes—because she has a special Force connection to animals. She wants to use those abilities to care for and treat creatures big and small.

KILDO

PRONOUNS: He/him
SPECIES: Alcedian
HEIGHT: 1.50 m (4 ft 11 in)

ALLEGIANCE: Jedi Order
FIRST APPEARANCE: EfV

Kildo is a mischievous youngling at the Valo Jedi outpost who enjoys using the Force to prank others. He retreats with his friends Gavi and Tep Tep into the mountains when the Nihil take over the planet. After hiding for months, the trio hear rumors of a mysterious vigilante named Scarlet Skull who is fighting back against the invaders. Kildo and his friends feel bolstered by this individual's brave acts, so they decide to return to the city.

NOOA

PRONOUNS: She/her
SPECIES: Urodel
HEIGHT: 1.68 m (5 ft 6 in)

ALLEGIANCE: Jedi Order
FIRST APPEARANCE: TfGE: LC

Nooa is an Urodel Jedi Padawan. She is inquisitive and eager to improve her lightsaber skills, but struggles with patience and control. She accompanies her master, Jedi Knight Ady Sun'Zee, to the planet Valron where Ady used to train with her late mentor, Master Sylwin.

Adhesive fingerpads

> "I MEAN I KNOW WE'RE PEACEKEEPERS, BUT HOW ARE WE SUPPOSED TO KEEP THE PEACE WITHOUT SOME MUSCLE?"
>
> – Nooa

DAGAN GERA

JEDI EXPLORER

Pale hair and eyes are a common Arkanian trait

Ornate gold lightsaber emitter

PRONOUNS: He/him
SPECIES: Arkanian offshoot
HEIGHT: 1.80 m (5 ft 11 in)

ALLEGIANCE: Jedi Order
FIRST APPEARANCE: J: S

Jedi Knight Dagan Gera is based on the Outer Rim planet Koboh. He and his partner, scientist Santari Khri, are part of a research team studying the strange element known as Koboh Matter. When they realize it is the same substance that forms the chaotic Koboh Abyss just beyond the planet's atmosphere, they decide to use Santari's technology to enable Dagan to fly the first mission through the Abyss to whatever lies beyond.

TANALORR TEMPLE
Beyond the Abyss, Dagan discovers a beautiful world that he names "Tanalorr." He records the journey on one of Santari's compasses so their Republic allies can follow. Dagan petitions the Jedi Order to set up a new temple outpost on Tanalorr where younglings can be trained, and construction begins. However, the Nihil manage to locate Tanalorr and attack the temple. Following the attack, the Jedi Council orders Dagan and Santari to abandon the planet and destroy Santari's compasses—the only way to reach the world. An incensed Dagan turns on his fellow Jedi and is defeated by Santari, who leaves him to heal in a bacta tank on Koboh.

"OUR TEMPLE WILL BE A BASTION FOR THE ORDER, HERE AT THE GALACTIC FRONTIER."

– Dagan Gera

SANTARI KHRI

NOTED JEDI SCIENTIST

Mission attire shows a commitment to field work

Datapad tracks Santari's research progress

PRONOUNS: She/her
SPECIES: Human
HEIGHT: 1.70 m (5 ft 7 in)

ALLEGIANCE: Jedi Order
FIRST APPEARANCE: J: S

Renowned scientist Santari Khri leads a team of Jedi and Republic researchers analyzing the unique properties of Koboh Matter, an element native to the Koboh system. Together with her partner, Jedi Dagan Gera, Santari builds huge ground-to-space arrays that clear a path through a space storm known as the Koboh Abyss. This allows the Jedi to locate the hidden world of Tanalorr, where they build a training outpost.

PARTNERS SEPARATED

When an Emergence—a chunk of falling space debris—comes out of hyperspace and shatters Koboh's moon, the ensuing disaster forces the Jedi and Republic to evacuate Koboh. Santari doesn't have enough time to travel to the facility where an injured Dagan is healing. Instead, she sends a trusted droid named ZN-A4 to wake him when it's safe. However, on its way, the droid is trapped by collapsing structures so, while Santari returns to Coruscant, Dagan remains behind on the abandoned planet.

Centuries later, prospectors and settlers who come to call Koboh home make use of Santari's scientific discoveries, which help them traverse and explore the planet.

> "IT'S HARD TO BELIEVE THIS PARADISE WAS WAITING ON JUST THE OTHER SIDE OF THE ABYSS!"
>
> – **Santari Khri**

KAI BRIGHTSTAR

PRONOUNS: He/him
SPECIES: Human
HEIGHT: 1.30 m (4 ft 3 in)

ALLEGIANCE: Jedi Order
FIRST APPEARANCE: YJA

Youngling Kai Brightstar trains along with his friends, Lys and Nubs, under Masters Yoda and Zia. Sometimes Kai wants to try things he may not be ready for, but it's only because he is eager to learn the ways of the Jedi. After experiencing failure, Kai grows to trust himself and the Force. When Kai loses his lightsaber on a mission, Yoda lets him use the lightsaber he used as a youngling many, many years ago.

"BREATHE, BE CALM, AND TRUST EACH OTHER."

— **Kai Brightstar**

Younglings wear robes similar to those of Padawans and Knights

Lightsaber held in classic training stance

Training lightsaber with low-power blade

Facial tattoos represent her Pantoran heritage

LYS SOLAY

PRONOUNS: She/her
SPECIES: Pantoran
HEIGHT: 1.20 m (3 ft 11 in)

ALLEGIANCE: Jedi Order
FIRST APPEARANCE: YJA

Lys Solay is a youngling training at the Jedi temple on the planet Tenoo. Together with her friends, Kai and Nubs, she works hard to learn the ways of the Force. While Lys likes to follow the rules, she is always willing to support her fellow younglings if one of them gets into trouble. Lys is proud to have a special connection with animals, especially the local wildlife on Tenoo.

"I'M LOOKING FOR A TOOKA KITTEN THAT ESCAPED. SEEN ONE?"

— **Lys Solay**

NUBS

PRONOUNS: He/him
SPECIES: Pooba
HEIGHT: 74 cm (2 ft 5 in)

ALLEGIANCE: Jedi Order
FIRST APPEARANCE: YJA

Nubs is small but super strong! He is in training to be a Jedi along with his friends, Kai and Lys. Nubs doesn't speak the same language as his pals, but he is very expressive so everyone can tell what's on his mind. He can be a bit clumsy at times, but he always bounces back. A lover of nature, Nubs has been known to get distracted by sweet-smelling plants during missions. But his friends know they can always count on him.

Ears are sensitive to high-pitched sounds

Blue lightsaber blade matches Nubs' fur

NASH DURANGO

PRONOUNS: She/her
SPECIES: Human
HEIGHT: 1.20 m (3 ft 11 in)

ALLEGIANCE: Galactic Republic
FIRST APPEARANCE: YJA

Nash Durango is the pilot of the *Crimson Firehawk* along with her droid copilot, RJ-83, who frequently rides on her shoulder. Filled with confidence after being trained to fly by both of her moms (who own a shuttle company), Nash loves speeding through space on her travels in the Outer Rim. She and RJ are good friends with many Jedi younglings who train at the temple on Tenoo, including Kai, Lys, and Nubs.

"YOU NEED ME TO FLY IN TO HELP OUT? YOUR TRUST PILOT IS READY."

– Nash Durango

RJ can tuck his arms under his domed head

Pockets carry extra supplies, just in case

CHAPTER TWO

THREATS TO THE JEDI

The Jedi of the High Republic find themselves battling pirates, outlaws, marauders, and monsters. Some threats linger at the edge of known Republic space, while others lie dormant for centuries until they are awakened once more.

PIRATES

The most pressing threat is the Nihil, a group of chaotic pirates. Each Nihil fights for plunder and for the respect (or fear) of their fellows. Eye of the Nihil, Marchion Ro, maintains his leadership because he has access to a mysterious source of precious hyperspace paths.

MONSTERS

Generations before the creation of Starlight Beacon, the Path of the Open Hand—a reclusive cult—discovers mysterious creatures that feed on the Force. Known as the Nameless, they are living weapons against Force-sensitive beings.

With a similarly insatiable appetite, the Drengir are a species of plantlike life-forms, which hunger for living prey. They have a strong connection to the dark side, which is passed down to them through a bond with their Progenitor.

CRIMINALS

A thriving trade exists among big gangs, small-time smugglers, outlaws, and thieves. Many of them will stop at nothing to continue their underworld activities. Although the Jedi are at the height of their power, the dark threats they face will always give them something to fear.

PATH OF THE OPEN HAND

The Jedi are far from the only group in the galaxy built around the Force. The Path of the Open Hand is a small cult that has settled on the planet Dalna. The lies of its leader, the Mother, lead the group to clash with the Jedi. Path members live simple lives, though the cult has one extravagance: its mighty flagship, the *Gaze Electric*.

BELIEFS ABOUT THE FORCE

Instead of finding their own unique way of understanding or connecting to the Force, Path members are forbidden entirely from using it. They accept its mystical power and revere it, but believe that using it—even to help others—will always lead to harm being done somewhere else. Since the Jedi tap into their connection to the Force so often, the Path considers them enemies who continually throw the Force out of balance and increase the amount of suffering in the galaxy.

Path members honor "gifts freely given," and they hand out small items such as flowers. They live low-tech lives in their communal home on Dalna, surrounded by farmland, which they tend. Families are celebrated and children are taught in groups by cult members.

A VIOLENT UNDERBELLY

The Path of the Open Hand is led by Elicia Zeveron, known to her followers as the Mother. She conceals from them the fact that she's mildly Force-sensitive, and she uses her abilities in secret to con her followers while

taking advantage of their generosity and support. Her second-in-command is the Herald, an intimidating Nautolan with a mysterious, violent past.

The Mother pretends to believe in the Path's laws. She says that avoiding use of the Force is an effort toward peace. At the same time, she stokes violence. She recruits some members of the cult into a group known as the Children. They steal valuable artifacts that are strong in the Force, and stockpile weapons. The Mother also has agents stationed throughout the galaxy. They encourage chaos that will benefit the Mother, such as the war between the planets Eiram and E'ronoh, which weakens the Jedi and the Republic.

Other members of the Path don't know what the Children do. In fact, no one in the Path knows the Mother's true origins until her Jedi sister, Oliviah, encounters them. Oliviah reveals that Elicia has been lying about her motives and concealing her own Force sensitivity.

LEGACY OF BLOOD

Discovering the truth about the Mother leads to the end of the Path of the Open Hand, though the influence of the cult on the galaxy continues even after it dissolves. True believer Marda Ro transforms it into the Path of the Closed Fist, which in turn inspires the formation of the Nihil. Generations later, a group known as the Elders of the Path will hold similar beliefs about the Force, and forbid its use among members.

THE MOTHER

PRONOUNS: She/her
SPECIES: Human
HEIGHT: 1.60 m (5 ft 3 in)

ALLEGIANCE: Path of the Open Hand
FIRST APPEARANCE: PoD

Elecia Zeveron transforms the Path of the Open Hand from a simple, frugal community into a powerful cult. But she is a con artist, out to gather as much wealth as she can for herself. She uses the Path to that end, impressing its members with her concealed Force abilities, which she uses to grow a lush garden during a lean season. Elecia calls herself "the Mother" and tells her new followers that she won't tolerate use of the Force by anyone. The Mother also forms the Children, a gang of young thieves within the cult. In secret, they collect Force artifacts for her, and Elecia's influence and wealth grows.

SHOWDOWN ON JEDHA
Forced to flee the planet Dalna in the cult's ship, the *Gaze Electric*, the Mother moves the Path of the Open Hand to Jedha. There, the Path clashes with the Convocation of the Force, a group that connects various Force sects. The Path's former leader, the Herald—now second-in-command to the Mother—pushes the Path to become more public and more violent.

Brikal shell blue face paint

Clothes are more elegant than those of her humble followers

TRUTH AND VENGEANCE

Eventually, the conflict between the Path of the Open Hand and the Convocation comes to a head and Elecia leaves the Herald behind. However, he is present later, when Elecia's sister, Jedi Knight Oliviah Zeveron, reveals that the Mother is a charlatan. Elecia's most loyal follower, Marda Ro, is present as well, and it is too much for her to take. She unleashes the Nameless creature known as the Leveler and lets it feed on the Mother, thus ending Elicia's reign.

"THE FORCE HAS SPOKEN."

– Elecia Zeveron

YANA RO

CONFLICTED PATH MEMBER

Green Children's tunic with concealed blaster strapped under her arm

Strong hands from farmwork and training

PRONOUNS: She/her
SPECIES: Evereni
HEIGHT: 1.70 m (5 ft 7 in)

ALLEGIANCE: Path of the Open Hand
FIRST APPEARANCE: PoD

Yana Ro and her cousin, Marda Ro, were brought to the Path of the Open Hand at a very young age, and enjoy the peaceful life it offers. Yana and her girlfriend, Kor Plouth, join the Children, a group of Path members chosen by their leader, the Mother. They steal Force artifacts, with Yana using her slicer skills to break into secure data terminals.

BEYOND THE LIES

Yana never believes in the Path's creed that the Force must not be used. She wants to leave one day and seek out a new life with Marda and Kor. But when Kor is killed on a mission and it is revealed that the Mother just wants the artifacts for her own gain, Yana starts to question everything.

"I BELONG OUT THERE, FREE TO FIND MY OWN DIRECTION."

– Yana Ro

MARDA RO

GUIDE OF THE PATH

Lompop flowers grow wild on Dalna

Thick wool cloak

Plain, homespun plain fabric

PRONOUNS: She/her
SPECIES: Evereni
HEIGHT: 1.68 m (5 ft 6 in)

ALLEGIANCE: Path of the Open Hand, Path of the Closed Fist
FIRST APPEARANCE: PoD

Marda Ro is a true believer in the Path of the Open Hand's mission. Raised in the cult from a young age, she never knew any other way. She sees the Path as a shelter from a world that hates and fears Evereni like herself. More innocent and impressionable than her cousin, Yana Ro, Marda wants to follow in Yana's footsteps and become one of the Children, a group she believes spreads the teachings of the Path to others. Marda has a brief romance with the Jedi Kevmo Zink. However, she steadfastly believes in the Path's philosophy that using the Force is wrong, and later blames the Jedi for his death.

"THE FORCE MUST BE FREE."

– Marda Ro

FORGING A NEW PATH

Marda eventually changes her mind about the Path when Yana convinces her that the Mother is a con artist who doesn't actually care about any of the members. Furious, Marda unleashes a Nameless, the Leveler, on the Mother. She then takes the Path's *Gaze Electric* flagship and heads out into space to fight against the Jedi. Years later, a descendent of hers is born, named Marchion Ro.

THE HERALD

THE FIST OF THE PATH

Head-tails damaged in a fight in the Herald's youth

Pack contains rations and holos of Kor and Opari

PRONOUNS: He/him
SPECIES: Nautolan
HEIGHT: 1.93 m (6 ft 4 in)

ALLEGIANCE: Path of the Open Hand
FIRST APPEARANCE: PoD

The Herald is the stern and serene second-in-command of the Path of the Open Hand. He is cold even in the face of great tragedy, and willing to hurt others to get what he wants. The Herald's mysterious past includes some time as the original leader of the Path. When the Mother joins, he willingly steps aside, impressed by her supposed healing abilities.

CONFLICT IN THE SECT

On Jedha, the Herald incites a huge riot on the steps of the Convocation of the Force and he clashes with the Jedi. Working with fellow Path member Yana Ro, he learns that the Mother lied to them and set up his daughter, Kor, to die. The Herald bides his time before openly attacking the Mother.

"IT IS IMPORTANT TO MAKE A HOME, TO HOLD SPACE, JUST AS IMPORTANT AS FIGHTING."

– The Herald

ENFORCER DROIDS

WAR MACHINES

TYPE: Combat droid
HEIGHT: 1.83 m (6 ft)
ALLEGIANCE: Path of
the Open Hand, Path
of the Closed Fist

FIRST APPEARANCE:
TBoJ

The Path of the Open Hand uses enforcer droids to attack its enemies and cause chaos during conflicts on both Dalna and Jedha. Tough and nimble, the droids can get back to their feet quickly after being knocked down. Their built-in arm blasters fire deadly bolts, and their strong armor can withstand multiple shots before the droid starts to falter.

"LAY DOWN YOUR WEAPONS OR YOU WILL BE DESTROYED."

– Enforcer droid

FRONTLINE MUSCLE
The Path ships enforcer droids to its Dalna compound hidden inside crates that are meant for storing rice. The droids join the cult's battle against the Jedi, and their durable armor and sheer numbers slow down the Jedi significantly. While most of these droids are destroyed, some remain in service to the Ro family. Around 150 years later, Marchion Ro uses the same kind of droids to crew his ship, the *Gaze Electric*.

Visual, audio, heat, and positioning sensors

Primary power coupler

Matrixed composite plating

ORANALLI

PRONOUNS: He/him
SPECIES: Dressellian
HEIGHT: 1.75 m (5 ft 9 in)

ALLEGIANCE: Temple of the Kyber
FIRST APPEARANCE: THR (PII)

Oranalli is an archivist at the Temple of the Kyber in the Holy City on Jedha. But he is secretly helping members of the Path of the Open Hand to steal artifacts. When local Padawan Matthea Cathley and visiting Jedi Vildar Mac come to report a relic they believe was stolen from the temple, Oranalli is quick to cover his tracks by laying the blame on former Guardian of the Whills Tey Sirrek. Oranalli's selfish ways eventually catch up with him. After the Battle of Jedha, Oranalli is betrayed and killed by the Herald of the Path of the Open Hand.

Specialized glasses help with cataloging and identifying relics and documents

"YOU WERE THE ONES WHO LOST THE ROD OF DAYBREAK AFTER I DELIVERED IT TO YOU ON A PLATTER."

– Oranalli to the Herald

BINNOT ULLO

PRONOUNS: He/him
SPECIES: Mirialan
HEIGHT: 1.88 m (6 ft 2 in)

ALLEGIANCE: Path of the Open Hand
FIRST APPEARANCE: Con

A member of the Path of the Open Hand and a faithful servant to the Mother, Binnot carries with him a secret—he is Force-sensitive. Binnot helps recruit Axel Greylark, son of Republic Chancellor Kyong Greylark, into the Path of the Open Hand when they are both teenagers. But Binnot grows deeply resentful of Axel's privileged life and how much interest the Mother shows in him. Always looking to gain more power and impress the Mother, Binnot carries out missions delivering bioweapons and enforcer droids. However, his disdain for Axel and his concealed Force abilities eventually lead to his downfall.

"YOU EITHER FIGHT, OR YOU'RE USELESS. THIS IS WHAT YOU ARE NEEDED FOR. THIS IS WHAT THE PATH ASKS. THE TIME OF PEACEFULLY GROWING CROPS AND LETTING THE REST OF THE GALAXY STEP ALL OVER OUR BELIEFS IS OVER."

– Binnot Ullo

FEL IX

PRONOUNS: He/him
SPECIES: Kessarine
HEIGHT: 1.63 m (5 ft 4 in)

ALLEGIANCE: Path of the Open Hand
FIRST APPEARANCE: PoD

Along with his partners, Er Dal and Ferize, Fel Ix is the loving parent of five hatchlings raised as part of the Path of the Open Hand. Though his partners and three of the hatchlings are rescued from a flooding cave by the Jedi Kevmo Zink, Fel Ix maintains his hatred of the Jedi. Later, the Mother assigns him to slice into Republic comms buoys. In the ensuing adventure, Jedi Rooper Nitani challenges Fel Ix's long-held beliefs about the Jedi. After getting to know Rooper, Fel Ix decides to leave the Path and its extreme beliefs, though he still remains spiritual and devoted to the Force.

> "WE BELIEVE THAT THE FORCE IS EVERYTHING."
>
> – Fel Ix

KOR PLOUTH

PRONOUNS: She/her
SPECIES: Nautolan
HEIGHT: 1.78 m (5 ft 10 in)

ALLEGIANCE: Path of the Open Hand
FIRST APPEARANCE: PoD

Kor Plouth is one of the Mother's Children, who steal Force artifacts for their cult, the Path of the Open Hand. Kor possesses mild Force sensitivity, which helps her identify such objects, and her acrobatic skills enable her to access those in hard-to-reach places. She is a devout member of the Path and, like her father, the Herald, she believes in the Mother's powers. Kor's own mother, Opari, is ill, and she trusts that the Mother will heal her. Kor also dreams of exploring the galaxy with her partner, Yana Ro, spreading the Path's creed on other planets. Kor's dreams, however, remain unfulfilled as she suffers an untimely death.

> "THE FORCE MUST BE FREE, AND I WANT TO BE FREE, TOO."
>
> – Kor Plouth

SHEA GANANDRA

PRONOUNS: She/her
SPECIES: Human
HEIGHT: 1.68 m (5 ft 6in)
ALLEGIANCE: Path of the Open Hand
FIRST APPEARANCE: THR (PII)

Engineer Shea Ganandra is recruited as a thief to the Children, a gang within the Path of the Open Hand. She travels with Marda Ro and prospector Radicaz "Sunshine" Dobbs to Planet X to collect Nameless eggs. After the Battle of Dalna, Ganandra leaves the Path, planning to raise her daughter and become a cargo hauler with Yana Ro.

"I'M REWRITING THE KNOWN LAWS OF HYPERSPACE UP HERE."

– Shea Ganandra

CINCEY

PRONOUNS: They/them
SPECIES: Human
HEIGHT: 1.68 m (5 ft 6 in)
ALLEGIANCE: Path of the Open Hand
FIRST APPEARANCE: PoD

Cincey manages the communications of the Path of the Open Hand—a big part of which means censoring the information that comes out of the cult's commune. As a member of the Children, Cincey steals Force artifacts along with Yana Ro, Kor Plouth, and Treze. Cincey uses a hover chair and is known for their short temper.

"THE FORCE WILL FORGIVE THE TRESPASS."

– Cincey

TREZE

PRONOUNS: He/him
SPECIES: Mikkian
HEIGHT: 1.65 m (5 ft 5 in)
ALLEGIANCE: Path of the Open Hand
FIRST APPEARANCE: PoD

Although Treze is a member of the Children, he doesn't believe in the group's extremist mission to stop all use of the Force across the galaxy. Aboard the Children's ship, the *Harmony*, he goes on Path missions to steal ancient artifacts. He is good-natured and flirtatious, leaving behind a distraught girlfriend when he is killed during a mission.

"IT WAS A GLORIOUS ACT. IN AND OUT BEFORE THEY WERE ANY THE WISER."

– Treze

OLD WAIDEN

PRONOUNS: He/him
SPECIES: Human
HEIGHT: 1.65 m (5 ft 5 in)
ALLEGIANCE: Path of the Open Hand
FIRST APPEARANCE: PoD

Old Waiden oversees the Path of the Open Hand's communal meals, cooking simple food for ceremonies such as the naming of new children. He is friendly with fellow Path member Marda Ro and has full faith in the Path's purpose. He knows that the Mother killed Jedi Kevmo Zink, and stands by her, firmly believing it was for the good of the Path.

"ARE YOU INJURED, MARDA?"

– Old Waiden

WOLE

PRONOUNS: He/him
SPECIES: Rodian
HEIGHT: 1.70 m (5 ft 7 in)

ALLEGIANCE: Path of the Open Hand
FIRST APPEARANCE: THRA: TNT

Wole is part of the Path of the Open Hand strike team led by Shalish. He asks Republic medic Ambar and Jedi Xenith Tarl to heal his friend, Geth, after a Nameless attack. After a while, Wole begins to doubt Shalish's leadership and befriends the Jedi Rok Buran.

FERIZE

PRONOUNS: She/her
SPECIES: Kessarine
HEIGHT: 1.68 m (5 ft 6 in)

ALLEGIANCE: Path of the Open Hand
FIRST APPEARANCE: PoD

Ferize raises her five hatchlings with her partners Fel Ix and Er Dal in the Path of the Open Hand commune on Dalna. Ferize calls for help from Marda Ro and Jedi Kevmo Zink when Er Dal and her hatchlings are trapped in their flooding home cave. When Fel Ix decides to leave the Path, she and Er Dal choose family over faith to join him.

"WE UNDERSTAND. FAMILY."

— Ferize

OPARI

PRONOUNS: She/her
SPECIES: Nautolan
HEIGHT: 1.65 m (5 ft 5 in)

ALLEGIANCE: Path of the Open Hand
FIRST APPEARANCE: PoD

Opari is the partner of the Herald, the Path's second-in-command, and mother to their daughter, Kor Plouth. Opari is sick with a disease, for which she soaks in brine and takes treatments recommended by the Mother. When feeling well enough, she enjoys seeing fellow Path members such as Yana Ro at community events.

"YANA, THANK YOU FOR ALL YOUR HARD WORK."

— Opari

ER DAL

PRONOUNS: He/him
SPECIES: Kessarine
HEIGHT: 1.57 m (5 ft 2 in)

ALLEGIANCE: Path of the Open Hand
FIRST APPEARANCE: PoD

Er Dal is a Kessarine member of the Path of the Open Hand, known for his foraging skills. After nearly six weeks inside their nesting cell, Er Dal and his partners, Ferize and Fel Ix, emerge with five children. The proud parents are all members of the Path, and each baby is initiated into the group during a naming ceremony. When a disaster traps him and some of his family in their home, Er Dal struggles valiantly to protect them until they are rescued by Jedi Kevmo Zink and Path member Marda Ro.

DELWIN

PRONOUNS: He/him
SPECIES: Weequay
HEIGHT: 1.88 m (6 ft 2 in)

ALLEGIANCE: Path of the Open Hand
FIRST APPEARANCE: PoD

One of the Path of the Open Hand's Elders, Delwin is present when fellow Path member Marda Ro asks the Mother permission to spread the teachings of the Path on Jedha. Delwin's surprise shows on his usually unreadable face, and he asks Marda for details about her plan. He later goes along when the Path flees from Dalna to Jedha.

"TWO EVERENI WILL HARDLY REMAIN UNNOTICED IN A PLACE LIKE JEDHA."

– Delwin, about Marda and Yana Ro

NADDIE

PRONOUNS: She/her
SPECIES: Human
HEIGHT: 1.07 m (3 ft 6 in)

ALLEGIANCE: Path of the Open Hand
FIRST APPEARANCE: TBoJ

Naddie is one of the children under Marda Ro's care when the Path of the Open Hand arrives on Jedha. Naddie releases a group of predatory wargarans from their cages because she believes they should be free. The animals attack her, and Marda rescues her before she is seriously hurt. Naddie is left with scars.

"THE FORCE WILL BE FREE!"

– Naddie

KANE

PRONOUNS: He/him
SPECIES: Weequay
HEIGHT: 1.68 m (5 ft 6 in)

ALLEGIANCE: Path of the Open Hand
FIRST APPEARANCE: THRA: TNT

Path member Kane believes that the Jedi are pompous, arrogant, and hypocritical, and he is eager to destroy them. He goes toe to toe with Jedi Coron Solstus while the Nameless attack both the Jedi and the Path. Kane almost overpowers Coron, but he is subdued by Jedi Master Rok Buran.

SHALISH

PRONOUNS: She/her
SPECIES: Human
HEIGHT: 1.68 m (5 ft 6 in)

ALLEGIANCE: Path of the Open Hand
FIRST APPEARANCE: THRA: TNT

Shalish leads the Path strike team that confronts the crew of the Republic ship *Witherbloom*. At first she attacks the Jedi and mocks their kindness toward others, but she later agrees that her wounded friend Geth needs Jedi help. Unfortunately for Shalish, the Nameless creature she is transporting eventually ends her life.

SACHAR ROLD

PRONOUNS: He/him
SPECIES: Unknown
HEIGHT: 1.78 m (5 ft 10 in)

ALLEGIANCE: Path of the Open Hand
FIRST APPEARANCE: PoD

Sachar Rold is the founder of the Path of the Open Hand. A former Guardian of the Whills, he disagreed with that group's beliefs about the Force and so created his own commune devoted to refraining from Force use instead. Rold claims to have seen a vision of a vivid blue light, which guided him to Dalna and led him to set up the Path in a place he believed would protect its members from the war and pain he'd experienced on Jedha. Later, when she first approaches the Path, the Mother lies that she saw a similar vision, lending legitimacy to her rise to power.

REGNAR PULIP

PRONOUNS: He/him
SPECIES: Human
HEIGHT: 1.73 m (5ft 8 in)

ALLEGIANCE: Path of the Open Hand
FIRST APPEARANCE: PoD

Regnar Pulip is the Path of the Open Hand's richest and most reliable backer. He funds many of the cult's basic needs, and also provides for the shadier expenses required by the Children. The Children are a secret group of thieves within the Path who work for the Mother, helping her locate and steal powerful artifacts that are strong in the Force. Pulip's vast wealth gives him enormous influence, which he uses to support select people throughout the galaxy.

TROMAK

PRONOUNS: He/him
SPECIES: Gran
HEIGHT: 1.60 m (5 ft 3 in)

ALLEGIANCE: Path of the Open Hand, Elders of the Path
FIRST APPEARANCE: THRA (PI)

Tromak was raised in the Path of the Open Hand and is now a member of the Elders of the Path. Marchion Ro seeks him out for his knowledge of Force artifacts, but Tromak chooses to bargain with the Jedi, suggesting he knows the location of the Rod of Seasons, an artifact that can control the Leveler.

> "IT IS SACRED KNOWLEDGE!"
> – Tromak

BARBATASH

PRONOUNS: He/him
SPECIES: Unknown
HEIGHT: 2.08 m (6 ft 10 in)

ALLEGIANCE: Elders of the Path
FIRST APPEARANCE: RtCT

Barbatash is one of the leaders of the Elders of the Path, an anti-Jedi sect. His group resides on the planet Trymant IV when the Great Disaster hits. Zeen Mrala, a former member who chose to leave and embrace her Force abilities with the Jedi, recognizes Barbatash. He's willing to work with the Jedi and points Zeen in the direction of a nearby Nihil base.

> "LET ME HANDLE THESE INTRUDERS."
> – Barbatash

THE NIHIL

While the Republic and Jedi explore the vast reaches of space, a hidden threat lurks in the unknown. The Nihil are pirates with a secret weapon: they have access to hyperspace paths that are unknown to anyone else. This allows them to sneak up on their prey and emerge from space unexpectedly and (usually) violently, before vanishing completely. Led by the ruthless and ambitious Marchion Ro, the Nihil are driven by a love of bloodshed and chaos. When not out raiding in their various starships, they party their days away at their base, the space station known as the Great Hall of the Nihil.

PLUNDER AND SPICE

All members of the Nihil want the same things: money and loot. They prey on unsuspecting space travelers, intercepting and breaching their victims' ships. Then they stun the crew with gas and steal or ransack their way from there. A few Nihil serve the group in other ways. Dr. Kisma Uttersond earns his keep by caring for the elderly Mari San Tekka, scientist Zadina Mkampa invents cruel weapons, and some Nihil members go undercover for long periods of time before completing their missions of espionage, assassination, or sabotage.

RIDING THE STORM

Although the day-to-day life of the Nihil is wild and chaotic, there is some order. Marchion Ro, known as the Eye of the Nihil, rules the Nihil. He delegates to three lieutenants known as the Tempest Runners. Each Tempest Runner commands a fleet of ships led by squadron leaders called Storms. Below them are Nihil fighters known as Clouds and new recruits called Strikes. These underlings make up the bulk of the Nihil forces.

The higher in rank each Nihil is, the more they are respected and the larger a cut of the plunder they get. This structure breeds rivalry, which means most members are as wary of

their fellow Nihil as they are of their enemies. Marchion Ro keeps a tight hold of his position as Eye, keeping the precious hyperspace paths close to his chest to retain his power and advantage over the rest.

ETERNAL ENEMIES

Where the Jedi and Republic rely on order, the Nihil thrive on chaos. The sight of a Nihil starship is enough to cause fear on any ship or world in the galaxy. The Nihil resent the Republic and hate the Jedi. They plot and scheme to undermine their enemies in a myriad ways: infiltration by spies, unleashing deadly monsters, and relentless, regular raids. They also attack gatherings, such as the Republic Fair on Valo, and locations, including Starlight Beacon.

MARCHION RO

EYE OF THE NIHIL

PRONOUNS: He/him
SPECIES: Evereni
HEIGHT: 1.88 m (6 ft 2 in)

ALLEGIANCE: Nihil
FIRST APPEARANCE: LotJ

Marchion Ro leads the Nihil from the bridge of his flagship, the *Gaze Electric*. He and his father, Asgar Ro, transformed the Nihil from a small gang of pirates to a large fleet of marauders who spread terror across the galaxy. Marchion is known and feared as much for his intimidating mask as for his ruthless battle tactics. Although he is cruel and vengeful, Marchion is not blinded by anger. He plans his goals carefully and uses intrigue as often as force.

SECRETIVE SCHEMES

Marchion is behind many underhanded plots that help him grow in power and spread his influence far and wide. He works with undercover traitor Ghirra Starros, a Republic senator. He keeps the ancient Mari San Tekka alive in a medical pod and pretends to be in league with the Republic so Mari will share her secret knowledge of unmapped hyperspace lanes. Meanwhile, he keeps his three fleet leaders—known as Tempest Runners—competitive by causing them to constantly fight among themselves. Marchion imprisons Jedi Master Loden Greatstorm and oversees the large-scale Nihil attack on the Republic Fair on Valo. And it was Marchion who planned the Great Disaster, causing the destruction of *Legacy Run*.

THE NAMELESS

Marchion's family holds knowledge of ancient weapons, including the Nameless. These mysterious creatures can overwhelm Force-sensitive beings. Marchion retrieves one of the few known Nameless from secret ice caves on the planet Rystan. He brings this Nameless—known as the Great Leveler—into the wider galaxy for the first time, and releases it on the planet Grizal. This proves devastating for the Jedi, who are affected badly by the powers of the Nameless. Jedi Loden Greatstorm, a captive on the planet, is the first Jedi to die. Under Marchion's control, the Leveler turns many other Jedi into stone husks.

Needles of poison are concealed in gauntlets

Nihil mask protects against poison gas

Modified Evereni hunting rifle

"EVERYTHING AND EVERYONE IS A TOOL. I WILL USE THEM HOWEVER I NEED."

– Marchion Ro

VOICES FROM THE PAST

Throughout his life, Marchion is haunted by the voice of his deceased father, Asgar Ro. Marchion never got along with his father, who was the previous Eye of the Nihil. Marchion believed his father never brought the Nihil to their full cruel potential, while Asgar often belittled his son. Much of Marchion's chaotic ambition is driven by his father's greed, as well as an old grudge against the Jedi and Republic. As Marchion leads the Nihil into more dangerous battles, the voice of Asgar's memory cautions that the Leveler is too powerful for even Marchion to control, perhaps unstoppable. But whether Marchion will heed the warnings of his dead father, only time will tell.

Boots with magnetized soles for space travel

PRONOUNS: She/her
SPECIES: Twi'lek
HEIGHT: 1.68 m (5 ft 6 in)

ALLEGIANCE: Herself
FIRST APPEARANCE: LotJ

Lourna Dee is a Nihil Tempest Runner known for her cruelty. Her ship, the *Lourna Dee*, is named after the one person she trusts in the galaxy—herself. Guarded and secretive, she and her crew never say more than is necessary to outsiders, and they are always scheming to stay one step ahead of everyone else. Lourna will double-cross anyone to gain more power. She is watchful of her fellow Tempest Runners, ensuring that there are no plans to challenge the Nihil Eye Marchion Ro—unless she is involved in them.

BETRAYAL

As a young Twi'lek, Lourna is part of the first family of the colony world Aaloth. Her boyfriend stages a coup against her father and sells Lourna to Zygerrian criminals. The Jedi rescue her and encourage her to enroll in the Carida Military Academy. But Lourna grows frustrated there and takes off in a stolen starfighter. She crosses paths with Nihil Tempest Runner Pan Eyta, and Lourna ends up joining the group of marauders, who later help her exact revenge on her ex-boyfriend on Aaloth.

RISING UP THE RANKS

Lourna's successes see her promoted again and again within the Nihil organization, drawing the attention of the Eye, Marchion Ro. Lourna's influence enables her to convince Marchion to approve a mission to abduct the wealthy Blythe family for ransom. During the raid, Lourna captures a valuable prisoner, Jedi Master Loden Greatstorm. She brings him to Marchion, who holds him captive on his ship.

ALWAYS SCHEMING

Lourna has no problem going behind Marchion's back to improve her own situation. She recruits hyperspace scientist Chancey Yarrow to work on

Blast boxes amplify the power of Lourna's weapon

Mask filters poisonous toxins that incapacitate enemies

a gravity-well projector for the Nihil. But what Marchion doesn't know is that Lourna's true objective is to manipulate *him* into lending her his most prized possession—the person who provides Marchion with hyperspace paths.

Lourna later leads the Nihil attack on the Republic Fair on Valo, where she seeks the death of Chancellor Lina Soh. Due to her visibility during the attack, Lourna is presumed to be the leader of the Nihil, which eventually brings her to the attention of Jedi Master Avar Kriss.

Leather suit made from kell dragon hide

"DO YOU HEAR THAT, UNIVERSE? NO ONE IS EVER GOING TO TELL ME WHAT TO DO AGAIN! NO ONE!"

— Lourna Dee

DARING ESCAPE

On Xais, Lourna releases a Nameless creature on the Jedi Keeve Trennis and Terec to see the effects the monster has on them. Soon after, Avar Kriss tracks Lourna to the Nihil's secret hideout in No-Space. Lourna loses a hand in battle with Avar and is captured. However, the chaos resulting from an explosion on Starlight Beacon gives Lourna a chance to escape. She overwhelms Jedi OrbaLin before stealing the *Ataraxia* and disappearing into space.

PAN EYTA

CRUEL TEMPEST RUNNER

High-powered blaster rifle

PRONOUNS: He/him
SPECIES: Dowutin
HEIGHT: 2.59 m (8 ft 6 in)

ALLEGIANCE: Nihil
FIRST APPEARANCE: LotJ

As a Tempest Runner, Pan Eyta is one of Marchion Ro's three most powerful (and most competitive) lieutenants. From his flagship, the *Elegencia*, he commands a Tempest of ships full of pirates who tend to be similar to him—put-together and particular, even as they create chaos. Pan has made a name for himself for his habit of killing his enemies.

RACE TO THE BOTTOM

While Pan resents Marchion Ro's "easy" path to Nihil leadership, he often feuds with fellow Tempest Runners, including Lourna Dee, for Ro's approval and support. Pan, however, isn't one for playing nice, and he clashes with Ro enough that the Nihil leader poisons him. Ultimately it's rivalry with his supposed allies that destroys Pan, when his death comes by Lourna's hand.

> "REMEMBER, THE OBJECTIVE IS TO CAUSE AS MUCH DAMAGE AS POSSIBLE."
>
> – Pan Eyta

KASSAV MILLIKO

PRONOUNS: He/him
SPECIES: Weequay
HEIGHT: 1.68 m (5 ft 6 in)

ALLEGIANCE: Nihil
FIRST APPEARANCE: LotJ

Kassav Milliko has served the Nihil since the days of Marchion Ro's father. He runs his Tempest from the bridge of the *New Elite*, keeping a delicate balance of power among his pirates even while indulging in more cruelty than the Nihil are known for. Kassav directs his fleet to the planet Eriadu, where he forces the governor to pay them to destroy dangerous space debris. But Kassav's crew destroys Eriadu's moon instead. Marchion punishes Kassav, and Kassav decides to sell out the Nihil to Eriadu. Before Kassav can switch sides, though, Eriadu's governor shoots him dead.

> "WE'RE GONNA TAKE 'EM FOR EVERYTHING THEY'VE GOT, AND THEY'LL BE HAPPY WE DID."
> – **Kassav Milliko**

KARA XOO

PRONOUNS: She/her
SPECIES: Quarren
HEIGHT: 1.75 m (5 ft 9 in)

ALLEGIANCE: Nihil
FIRST APPEARANCE: AToC

Kara Xoo is the pirate captain of the ship *Poisoned Barb*. After Pan Eyta's death, she takes over as one of Marchion Ro's three Tempest Runners. Kara is always on the lookout for traitors, and she takes care to never show weakness to other Nihil. Among both the Nihil and their enemies she's known for bragging, torture, and destruction. Kara confers with Marchion on important strategic decisions, and she also oversees the kidnapping of children as new Nihil recruits—including genius inventor Avon Starros, who later escapes with her Jedi friend Vernestra Rwoh.

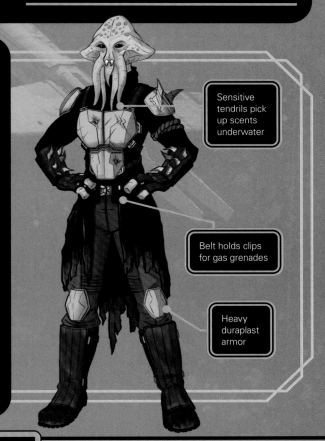

Sensitive tendrils pick up scents underwater

Belt holds clips for gas grenades

Heavy duraplast armor

Krix shaves his hair after joining the Nihil

PRONOUNS: He/him
SPECIES: Human
HEIGHT: 1.65 m (5 ft 5 in)

ALLEGIANCE: Elders of the Path, Nihil
FIRST APPEARANCE: THRA (PI)

Krix Kamerat was brought up believing that Force users are evil. When his close friend Zeen Mrala uses her hidden Force powers to protect their planet, Trymant IV, Krix cannot move past his sense of betrayal. He joins the Nihil and embraces the life of a marauder.

DESCENT INTO EVIL

Krix lets his anger toward Zeen grow into a quest to find ways to defeat the Jedi. As a Nihil cell leader, Krix pledges his allegiance to Marchion Ro. To prove he is worthy of Ro's trust, Krix leads a mission to Takodana in an attempt to destroy the Jedi temple there.

"NO ONE. SHE'S NO ONE TO ME."

– Krix Kamerat about Zeen Mrala

HOSNIAN PRIME SENATOR

Gold medallion necklace received upon becoming a senator

Green senatorial robes

PRONOUNS: She/her
SPECIES: Human
HEIGHT: 1.68 m (5 ft 6 in)

ALLEGIANCE: Nihil, Galactic Republic
FIRST APPEARANCE: OotS

Ghirra Starros is a Galactic Republic senator from Hosnian Prime, but she leads a secret double life. Publicly she works on Republic matters concerning hyperspace lanes, but privately she works with the Nihil—a secret she keeps even from her daughter, Avon. As a Nihil spy, Ghirra informs them of Republic news and sows discord in the Senate.

DANGEROUS GAMES
Seeking a closer relationship with the Eye of the Nihil, Marchion Ro, Ghirra sends him the plans of Starlight Beacon, which leads to its destruction. In the months after, Ghirra becomes the face of the Nihil in the Senate. She keeps an eye on her Nihil rivals while making plans for her own future.

> "YOU SHOULD'VE JUST DONE AS YOU WERE TOLD."
> – Ghirra Starros to Ghal Tarpfen

CUTTHROAT MERCENARY

Cloak shrouds face to give Viess a sense of menace

Beskar strips reinforce armor

PRONOUNS: She/her
SPECIES: Mirialan
HEIGHT: 1.68 m (5 ft 6 in)

ALLEGIANCE: Mercenary army
FIRST APPEARANCE: THR: TB

General Viess will fight anyone for money. She claims to have killed Jedi and, as she heads a mercenary army, no one is foolish enough to voice any doubts. Even though she hasn't earned enough to afford a full set of beskar armor, Viess wears an outfit plated with strips of the material, which will protect her against lightsaber strikes if she's careful.

NO HONOR
General Viess aids the Bethune army in their siege on the planet Gansevor, but Jedi partners Porter Engle and Barash Silvain return fire. Viess duels Porter but she doesn't fight honorably, tossing grenades into the crowd before fleeing. She later leads her army to ransack the devastated city.

"WHO AM I HERE TO KILL?"
– General Viess

PRONOUNS: He/him
SPECIES: Ithorian
HEIGHT: 1.96 m (6 ft 5 in)

ALLEGIANCE: Nihil
FIRST APPEARANCE: PoV

Baron Boolan was once a child raised by the Path of the Open Hand, where Marda Ro and other Path members taught him that use of the Force is evil and that only the Path knows the truth. These beliefs stay with him throughout his life.

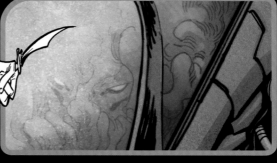

NAMELESS EXPERIMENTS

By the time Marchion Ro becomes Eye of the Nihil, Boolan has developed a reputation as a genius at physical manipulation, a talent he uses during his experiments. Along with his "Children of the Storm," Boolan specializes in working on the Nameless, and has learned to control them enough to force them to attack his enemies at will. He is one of three beings appointed by Marchion Ro as his Tempests after the fall of Starlight Beacon.

"THE MOTHER SAID THIS WAS THE ONLY WAY."
– Baron Boolan

SABATA KRILL

PRONOUNS: She/her
SPECIES: Er'Kit
HEIGHT: 1.65 m (5 ft 5 in)

ALLEGIANCE: Nihil
FIRST APPEARANCE:
THRA (PI)

Sabata Krill is a ruthless member of the Nihil, ready to double-cross anyone to make a name for herself. As part of Krix Kamerat's cell, Sabata pretends to defect from the Nihil on the planet Takodana. But it's just part of a plan for her to get inside the Takodana Jedi temple so she can plant a bomb. Later, Sabata continues to wreak havoc on the planet Corellia, where she helps the Nihil infiltrate the local police force.

> "DO YOU WANT TO WATCH YOUR PRETTY LITTLE SPACE STATION GET DESTROYED?"
>
> – Sabata Krill

ZADINA MKAMPA

Fire- and acid-resistant fabric

Cybernetic augmentations replace damaged face and arm

PRONOUNS: She/her
SPECIES: Human
HEIGHT: 1.70 m (5 ft 7 in)

ALLEGIANCE: Nihil
FIRST APPEARANCE: MtD

Scientist Zadina Mkampa builds weapons for Nihil commander Kara Xoo. Part of her work includes developing gas bombs and a machine to start groundquakes. When the Nihil kidnap a group of children, Mkampa forces one of them—young genius Avon Starros—to work with her. However, Avon sabotages the Nihil machines and uses the chaos to rescue the other kidnapped children.

> "WE HAVE TO EARN OUR KEEP."
>
> – Zadina Mkampa

NAN

PRONOUNS: She/her
SPECIES: Human
HEIGHT: 1.50 m (4 ft 11 in)

ALLEGIANCE: Nihil, Graf family
FIRST APPEARANCE: ItD

Left in the care of a Nihil named Hague after her parents' deaths, Nan grows up a marauder. She uses her deceptive skills to trick Jedi Reath Silas into trusting her on the Amaxine station, before betraying him. Although she is tempted to work with Chancey Yarrow for the Graf family, Nan remains convinced that the Nihil are her best bet for survival.

> "IN TIME, YOU WILL BOW BEFORE THE NIHIL."
>
> – Nan

CHANCEY YARROW

PRONOUNS: She/her
SPECIES: Human
HEIGHT: 1.63 m (5 ft 4 in)

ALLEGIANCE: Nihil, Byne Guild
FIRST APPEARANCE: OotS

Studying hyperspace theories at the Academy of Carida, Chancey Yarrow becomes obsessed with the idea of a machine that can pull ships out of hyperspace. After being expelled from the academy, Chancey later takes the extreme step of faking her own death so she can secretly work with the Nihil to build an artificial gravity well. Chancey's work separates her from her daughter, Sylvestri, who believes her mother to be a simple shipping hauler. Chancey meets her end on board Starlight Beacon after it is sabotaged by the Nihil. She tries to save lives by helping to repair the station, but she is killed by Jedi Elzar Mann, who thinks she's one of the Nihil bombers.

Mask protects her during Nihil gas attacks

> "WHO ELSE WOULD I WANT AT MY SIDE BUT MY DAUGHTER?"
>
> – Chancey Yarrow

Prefers to go barefoot

SHALLA RO

PRONOUNS: She/her
SPECIES: Evereni
HEIGHT: 1.65 m (5 ft 5 in)

ALLEGIANCE: Nihil
FIRST APPEARANCE:
THR: EotS

Shalla Ro leads the Nihil. The group was founded by her mother, who saw the pirates as the end point of hard-won Evereni survival. Shalla excels at making contacts and commanding lesser scoundrels to do her bidding. She is cautious and strategic as she tries to build her small gang into something more. Shalla is careful not to reveal the Nihil to the wider galaxy too quickly. For this reason, she hesitates to overuse her captive Mari San Tekka's new hyperspace paths. This puts her in conflict with her son, Asgar, who decides that he would make a better, more decisive leader of the Nihil—so he pushes Shalla to her death.

> "ALL OF OUR PEOPLE WHO SURVIVED THE GALAXY'S ATTEMPTS TO DESTROY OUR SPECIES ARE BLADES."
>
> – Shalla Ro

Ro family heirloom

ASGAR RO

PRONOUNS: He/him
SPECIES: Evereni
HEIGHT: 1.83 m (6 ft)

ALLEGIANCE: Nihil
FIRST APPEARANCE: TRS

Asgar Ro becomes the first Eye of the Nihil after he takes the leadership from his mother, Shalla. Unlike Shalla, who wanted to grow the Nihil stealthily, Asgar expands quickly, turning the small band of pirates into a large—and much feared—organization. One of Asgar's Tempest Runners, Lourna Dee, tries to form a partnership with him at the top of the Nihil chain. Instead, Asgar outlines his plan to keep all of the power for himself. Later, Lourna stabs him, ending Asgar's reign and unknowingly opening the way for his son, Marchion, to rise to power.

Ancient Evereni armor insulates against lightning

> "I'M A MAN WITH VISION."
>
> – Asgar Ro

ZAGYAR

PRONOUNS: He/him
ALLEGIANCE: Nihil
SPECIES: Human
FIRST APPEARANCE: LotJ
HEIGHT: 1.70 m (5 ft 7 in)

Zagyar is a Storm who leads a raiding party of Nihil pirates. Many of his crewmates die during the Great Disaster, when they mistakenly target a ship's fuel canister. Zagyar accompanies Marchion Ro to Trymant IV to kidnap Tromak, a cult member who has information about an ancient artifact Marchion is searching for.

TASIA

PRONOUNS: She/her
ALLEGIANCE: Nihil
SPECIES: Cathar
FIRST APPEARANCE: TR
HEIGHT: 1.65 m (5 ft 5 in)

Tasia is a Nihil Storm who is imprisoned along with her Tempest Runner, Lourna Dee, on the Republic ship *Restitution*. Tasia blackmails Lourna, threatening to reveal her identity after Lourna gives a fake name on arrest. Tasia later betrays Lourna to the Nihil Pan Eyta.

"IMAGINE THE BRAGGING RIGHTS."

— Tasia

SARN STARBREAKER

PRONOUNS: He/him
ALLEGIANCE: Nihil
SPECIES: Gloovan
FIRST APPEARANCE: TRS
HEIGHT: 1.88 m (6 ft 2 in)

Nihil Sarn Starbreaker is seeking a promotion to Storm. In an attempt to impress his boss, Tempest Runner Pan Eyta, he attacks the well-known Cyclor Shipyards, targeting the Republic's new research vessel, the *Innovator*. The barrage causes damage but does not destroy the *Innovator*.

"TARGET THE SHIPYARD AND FIRE."

— Sarn Starbreaker

MUGLAN

PRONOUNS: She/her
ALLEGIANCE: Nihil (formerly)
SPECIES: Gloovan
FIRST APPEARANCE: TR
HEIGHT: 1.83 m (6 ft)

Muglan is the bodyguard of the criminal Ola Hest. They are both former Hutt enforcers, now in the Republic prison. Hest develops a rivalry with fellow inmate Lourna Dee, and Muglan often gets put in the middle. After Lourna helps Muglan escape, she joins the Nihil as part of her Tempest.

MELIS SHRYKE

PRONOUNS: She/her
SPECIES: Unknown
HEIGHT: 1.68 m (5 ft 6 in)

ALLEGIANCE: Nihil
FIRST APPEARANCE: TEoD

Cruel captain Melis Shryke leads the crew of the Nihil ship the *Cacophony*. Her highly polished, deep-blue armor and shocking white hair make her a memorable sight even before she attacks her enemies. Shryke works for General Viess, one of Marchion Ro's lieutenants after the fall of Starlight Beacon. Her hunting ground is the Occlusion Zone, the lawless region of space that is completely under Nihil control. Shryke's quick, opportunistic raids leave the people she preys upon too stunned and scared to fight back. That is, until she comes up against the Jedi.

KLINITH DA

PRONOUNS: She/her
SPECIES: Human
HEIGHT: 1.60 m (5 ft 3 in)

ALLEGIANCE: Nihil
FIRST APPEARANCE: AToC

Klinith Da and her partner, Gwishi, are Nihil spies sent to sabotage the Republic. They destroy the luxury ship *Steady Wing* and clash with Jedi Vernestra Rwoh and Imri Cantaros. Da enjoys causing destruction and chaos. She fears that if the Republic expands its reach, her Nihil pirate adventures will stop.

GWISHI

PRONOUNS: He/him
SPECIES: Aqualish
HEIGHT: 1.78 m (5 ft 10 in)

ALLEGIANCE: Nihil
FIRST APPEARANCE: AToC

Gwishi is the leader of his Nihil strike team, and is unusually calm for a pirate. He cautions his partner, Klinith Da, not to show when she's nervous. He and Klinith destroy the ship *Steady Wing* in an attempt to keep the Republic out of Nihil territory. However, they are captured by Jedi Vernestra Rwoh and Imri Cantaros.

ZEETAR

PRONOUNS: He/him
SPECIES: Talpini
HEIGHT: 1.22 m (4 ft)

ALLEGIANCE: Nihil
FIRST APPEARANCE: TRS

Zeetar becomes one of the Nihil's three Tempest Runners after the death of previous leader Kassav Milliko. Like the Nihil he commands, Zeetar is cruel and enjoys the chaos of pirate life. He battles the Jedi several times, including at the Valo Republic Fair. Eventually he meets defeat at the hands of an angry Jedi, Avar Kriss.

ZARET

PRONOUNS: He/him
SPECIES: Human
HEIGHT: 1.68 m (5 ft 6 in)

ALLEGIANCE: Nihil
FIRST APPEARANCE:
TEoB, V1

As an undercover Nihil agent, Zaret works to take down the Jedi outpost on Banchii. He is spotted by Jedi Lily Tora-Asi and her Padawan, Keerin Fionn, who believe he is one of the local villagers. As part of his mission, Zaret helps a farmer, Kooba, import Drengir seeds, leading to a Drengir invasion and an attack on the Jedi.

KISMA UTTERSOND

PRONOUNS: He/him
SPECIES: Chadra-Fan
HEIGHT: 1 m (3 ft 3 in)

ALLEGIANCE: Nihil
FIRST APPEARANCE: LotJ

Kisma Uttersond is the Nihil doctor who oversees Mari San Tekka, an elderly captive of the Nihil who provides them with precious hyperspace paths. Uttersond is one of the few Nihil willing to talk back to Marchion Ro, since he knows Mari's health is on the line. He might be a doctor, but Uttersond has a cruel side, which shows when he tortures the Jedi Master Loden Greatstorm.

HAGUE

PRONOUNS: He/him
SPECIES: Zabrak
HEIGHT: 1.80 m (5 ft 11 in)

ALLEGIANCE: Nihil
FIRST APPEARANCE: ItD

Nihil strategist Hague raises young pirate Nan after the deaths of her parents, who were his friends. Hague and Nan are on board the Amaxine space station during the Great Disaster, and they clash with Jedi Reath Silas, Orla Jareni, and Cohmac Vitus. During the fight, Reath opens an airlock near where Hague is standing, and the elderly pirate is sucked out into space.

"YOUR SORCERY CANNOT SAVE YOU."

— **Hague to Orla Jareni**

THAYA FERR

PRONOUNS: She/her
SPECIES: Human
HEIGHT: 1.65 m (5 ft 5 in)

ALLEGIANCE: Nihil
FIRST APPEARANCE: TFS

Thaya Ferr is one of the Nihil closest to the Eye, Marchion Ro. Ferr assigns jobs to the Nihil crew, skillfully keeping secrets or turning people against each other for the Eye's benefit. At the same time, she can slice into Republic communications systems to transmit messages from her boss. Above all, she wants to impress Marchion.

"SLICING INTO THE COMMUNICATIONS BUOYS COMPLETE."

— **Thaya Ferr**

DRENGIR

CARNIVOROUS PLANT CREATURES

SPECIES: Drengir
HEIGHT: Varies

ALLEGIANCE: None
FIRST APPEARANCE: ItD

The Drengir are sentient plants that have only one thing on their mind—food! They feast on any and all living things, preferably while their prey is still alive. Drengir enjoy scaring their victims, and they call out "Meat! Meat!" while hunting. Tentacles grab and trap their prey, entering their mouths and nostrils to poison them and suck out nutrients. Lightsaber strikes have little effect on Drengir, which makes them difficult for even the Jedi to kill. Nihil marauders take advantage of the Drengir's insatiable hunger and seed them throughout the galaxy as a strategic weapon against the Jedi.

ROOT-MIND
The Drengir's thoughts are connected so they communicate as one collective—a root-mind that wants to grow and take over its surroundings. Drengir target young or weak civilians, gaining strength so they can spread out and control more territory.

THE DRENGIR AWAKEN
When several ships land on the plant-covered, abandoned Amaxine space station, many of the travelers feel a sinister presence and experience disturbing visions. The Jedi on board remove statues from the station that they don't realize were put in place by the Sith years ago to keep the Drengir in a deep slumber. Once the spell is broken, the Drengir start hunting and

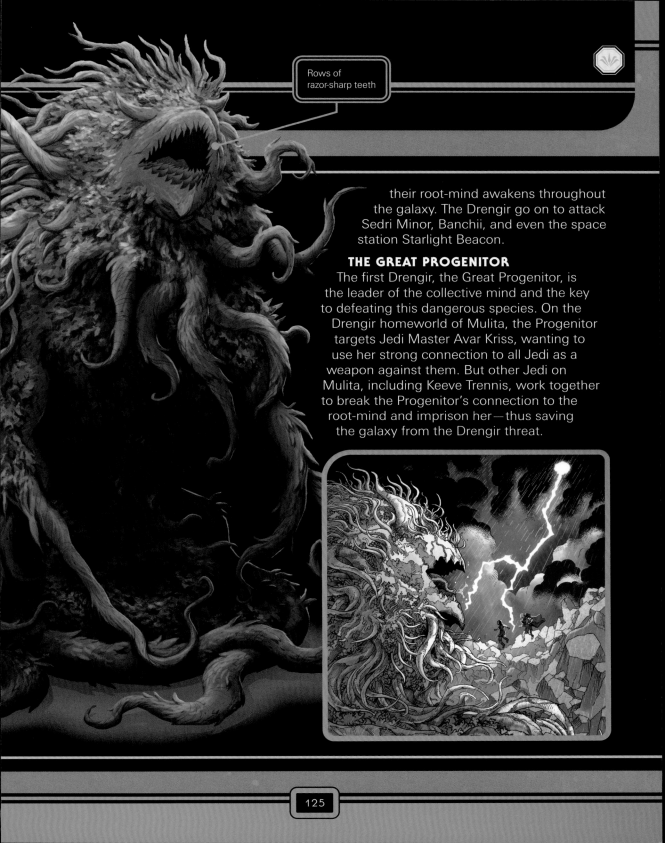

Rows of
razor-sharp teeth

their root-mind awakens throughout the galaxy. The Drengir go on to attack Sedri Minor, Banchii, and even the space station Starlight Beacon.

THE GREAT PROGENITOR

The first Drengir, the Great Progenitor, is the leader of the collective mind and the key to defeating this dangerous species. On the Drengir homeworld of Mulita, the Progenitor targets Jedi Master Avar Kriss, wanting to use her strong connection to all Jedi as a weapon against them. But other Jedi on Mulita, including Keeve Trennis, work together to break the Progenitor's connection to the root-mind and imprison her—thus saving the galaxy from the Drengir threat.

THE NAMELESS

FORCE EATERS

SPECIES: Nameless
HEIGHT: Varies

ALLEGIANCE: Path of
the Open Hand, Nihil
FIRST APPEARANCE: TRS

There are rumors that they come from a mysterious planet in Wild Space, but if anyone knows anything about it, it would seem they've kept it to themselves.

FORCE HUNGER
A Nameless attack can happen very slowly or all at once, but any Force user who comes into contact with a Nameless will eventually feel the effects of their hunger. First, a Force user will feel overwhelming, blinding confusion and terror. Then they'll experience terrifying visions as they struggle to perceive the physical form of the Nameless itself. These visions will likely be based on the Force user's insecurities, and can warp the appearance of the Nameless or the people around them. If the Force user doesn't escape at this point, they'll quickly become unable to move at all. In the final stage of a Nameless attack, the Force-sensitive victim will have their energy drained and their body completely transformed into a stonelike husk, which eventually crumbles into dust.

The dreaded Shrii-Ka-Rai have been the subject of Jedi legend since time immemorial. As children, Jedi Stellan Gios and Emerick Caphtor were sung a lullaby about them. The true nature of these creatures remains hidden for a long time, shrouded in myth, resulting in them becoming known as the monsters of bedtime stories, referred to as the "Nameless." What the Jedi learn is that the Nameless are ferocious beasts with an appetite for the Force.

Brightly burning eyes

Skeletal body

Tendrils spread feelings of terror and despair to Force-sensitive beings

THE NAMELESS AND THE PATH

Prospector Radicaz "Sunshine" Dobbs brings a Nameless egg to the Mother, who keeps it at her side. After hatching, the baby Nameless, deadly even in its bloblike early form, calcifies the Jedi Zallah Macri. Next, it solidifies into its fully-grown, four-legged shape.

The Mother and the Path of the Open Hand also come into possession of the Rod of Seasons, which can control the Nameless. Two other artifacts, the Rod of Ages and the Rod of Daybreak, are also known to exist.

REVIVAL

One hundred and fifty years later, when the Nameless are thought to be myth, Nihil leader Marchion Ro rediscovers his ancestors' shrine to the Nameless and retrieves one creature from where it has been frozen in ice. The Nihil unleash Nameless on the Jedi in numerous clashes, including on Starlight Beacon during its fall. Very few Jedi have proven able to survive a Force-depleting Nameless attack.

CHAPTER THREE

GALACTIC REPUBLIC

The Galactic Republic is a democratic body that governs planets throughout the galaxy. The elected Republic chancellors are tasked with keeping peace among its members, liaising with senators from member planets, and encouraging new worlds to join.

EXPLORATION AND COLLABORATION

During the High Republic era, the heart of the Republic lies in the Core Worlds—mainly Coruscant, Corellia, Alderaan, and Hosnian Prime. As trade routes and hyperspace travel expand and exploration teams head into the Outer Rim frontier, the reach and the influence of the Republic extends ever further. Co-chancellors Kyong Greylark and Orlen Mollo work to establish relationships with frontier worlds. Decades later, Chancellor Lina Soh makes a name for herself with her Great Works projects, including the space station Starlight Beacon, located at the edge of the Outer Rim—a symbol of the greatness of the Republic.

UNITED GALACTIC GOALS

The Republic and the Jedi Order join forces against galactic threats and work together on many initiatives, including Pathfinder teams, which are made up of both Jedi and Republic crew. While the Republic is made up of many different worlds, the goal of a unified galaxy remains a dream worth fighting for.

PATHFINDER TEAMS

The Galactic Republic is going through an age of growth and exploration. To aid these efforts, the Republic and Jedi Order combine their resources to create Pathfinder teams. The goal of these teams—consisting of Republic officers and Jedi—is to explore new worlds in the frontier, administer aid when needed, and improve communications to solidify relationships with civilizations who may one day join the Republic.

ADVENTURE AWAITS

A Pathfinder team typically includes five members: a Republic pilot, medic, and droid, and a Jedi Master and Padawan. Each should have a love of the unknown and be prepared for anything. It is crucial that Pathfinders trust one another completely because they will need to rely on their training and instincts when missions take them to worlds with dangerous terrain or inhabitants. The Jedi who lead the teams need to be masters in diplomacy, teamwork,

combat, and survival. Successful Pathfinder missions are publicly celebrated and the teams go down in history for their efforts.

WORKING TOGETHER

In many instances, Pathfinder teams reach remote locations where communications have not been set up. Because of these challenges, Pathfinder teams work closely with Republic communications teams, which are made up of two engineers and EX communication droids. As Pathfinder

Pilot Sallee Ooph

Team leader Jedi Master Helion Volte

Padawan Benj Marko

Astromech droid GT-22

Medic Grint Rupar

missions discover new worlds and travel routes, the comms team uses hyperspace buoys to install new comms lines. Once the systems are set up, the Jedi may choose to establish a permanent presence there, building outposts to act as bases for future missions.

SKILLED TEAM

The Jedi Master of a Pathfinder team has many roles. They serve as the team leader, as well as a teacher and mentor to their Padawan. The missions are inherently dangerous, so the bond between master and Padawan must be strong. Pilots must be skilled to fly in unknown terrain and able to repair their ship if it gets damaged. Medics need the confidence to give care despite being far from hospitals, and they are often called upon to help citizens they meet on missions, some of whom have anatomies different from anything they've seen before. GT astromech droids are the droid of choice for most Pathfinder teams. They help with repairs, scan items, and communicate with EX droids.

KYONG GREYLARK

CHANCELLOR OF THE REPUBLIC

Jadeite headdress is a family heirloom

Eiram seed pearls sewn into E'roni cupric ore thread

PRONOUNS: She/her
SPECIES: Human
HEIGHT: 1.63 m (5 ft 4 in)

ALLEGIANCE: Galactic Republic
FIRST APPEARANCE: Con

Chancellor Kyong Greylark spends more time on Coruscant than her co-chancellor, Orlen Mollo. Kyong is the one who handles the day-to-day affairs of the Republic Senate. She is savvy and skeptical, and doesn't take Orlen's or the Jedi Order's words at face value. Kyong believes in justice and discipline, and—with her Republic military academy training—she is not to be underestimated.

LETTING GO OF POWER
Kyong faces a tough decision during the Battle of Dalna. Her son, Axel, reveals that he is a member of the Path of the Open Hand, and that the Mother plans to use him as leverage to get to Kyong. Kyong's solution is to step down from her position as chancellor, removing any chance the Path has of gaining power by using her son against her.

"WRONGS MUST BE PAID FOR, EVEN IF HE IS MY ONLY CHILD."
– Kyong Greylark

ORLEN MOLLO

TRAVELING CHANCELLOR OF THE REPUBLIC

Decorative osmium buckle

Cloak is both formal and weatherproof

PRONOUNS: He/him
SPECIES: Quarren
HEIGHT: 1.88 m (6 ft 2 in)

ALLEGIANCE: Galactic Republic
FIRST APPEARANCE: Con

Chancellor Orlen Mollo is one of the two Republic leaders. While Kyong Greylark focuses on Coruscant and the Senate, Orlen—who believes himself more worldly—prefers to travel. His flagship, the *Paxion*, serves him well as a mobile base. Orlen keeps in touch with the Office of the Frontier and takes a personal interest in new hyperspace lanes.

EIRAM AND E'RONOH CONFLICT

Orlen believes the Republic shouldn't exert too strong an influence on nonmember planets. Because of this, he initially takes a watchful yet distant attitude to the war between Eiram and E'ronoh. But when the conflict escalates, Orlen convinces the two planets to work together. His blunt words and plea for peace prove to be just what the monarch of E'ronoh needs to hear.

"THE REPUBLIC WANTS PEACE MORE THAN ANYTHING."

– Orlen Mollo

DIETRIX JAGO

PRONOUNS: She/her
SPECIES: Unknown
HEIGHT: 1.70 m (5 ft 7 in)

ALLEGIANCE: Galactic Republic
FIRST APPEARANCE: QftHC

Described as endlessly enthusiastic by her coworkers, Dietrix Jago is a pilot on board the *Umberfall* and part of a Republic Pathfinder team led by Jedi Master Silandra Sho. Jago loves her ship and has a knack for repairing any part of it. She is easy to spot thanks to her rainbow hair, and is friends with her Jedi teammate Rooper Nitani.

"IF I SEE ANYTHING VAGUELY TERRIFYING, I'M PLANNING TO RUN AND HIDE."

– Dietrix Jago

ZZ-10

PRONOUNS: He/him
TYPE: ZZ droid
HEIGHT: 46 cm (1 ft 6 in)

ALLEGIANCE: Jedi Order
FIRST APPEARANCE: TEoB: P

ZZ-10 is a droid assigned to Jedi Master Ravna Abronsa. After the Battle of Dalna, ZZ-10 searches for Abronsa, initially unable to process that she has been killed. Later, he asks Abronsa's former Padawan, Arkoff, to bury him along with the journal of Jedi Azlin Rell in order to protect Rell's discoveries about the Nameless.

GT-11

PRONOUNS: He/him
TYPE: Astromech droid
HEIGHT: 1.17 m (3 ft 10 in)

ALLEGIANCE: Galactic Republic
FIRST APPEARANCE: QftHC

GT-11 is an astromech droid on the Republic Pathfinder mission led by Master Silandra Sho. Accused of being lazy by EX-9B, the other droid on the team, GT-11 welcomes the chance to take a break from the mission. He joins a Republic communications team on the planet Aubadas, helping to reestablish its disrupted comms system.

"WE'D BE DELIGHTED TO HAVE YOU, GEE-TEE!"

– Amos Tillian to GT-11

OBIK DENNISOL

PRONOUNS: He/him
SPECIES: Mirialan
HEIGHT: 1.70 m (5 ft 7 in)

ALLEGIANCE: Galactic Republic
FIRST APPEARANCE: QftHC

Obik Dennisol serves as the medic for the Pathfinder team on the *Umberfall*. As with other Mirialans, Dennisol's facial tattoos serve as a record of his achievements. Dennisol uses his scientific mind to help the local Katikoot population on the planet Gloam, who are being harmed by the effects of certain minerals.

"I MAY NOT BE TOUCHED BY THE FORCE BUT I KNOW THAT SOMETHING'S OFF HERE."

– Obik Dennisol

SALLEE OOPH

PRONOUNS: She/her
SPECIES: Human
HEIGHT: 1.68 m (5 ft 6 in)

ALLEGIANCE: Galactic Republic
FIRST APPEARANCE: THR: TB

Sallee Ooph is the pilot on Master Helion Volte's Pathfinder team, who are tasked with expanding the Republic comms network. Jedi Porter Engle and Barash Silvain ask her team for help, and Ooph transports the Jedi to Gansevor on her ship.

> "NICE TO GET A LITTLE RECOGNITION."
>
> – Sallee Ooph

GRINT RUPAR

PRONOUNS: He/him
SPECIES: Britarro
HEIGHT: 1.88 m (6 ft 2 in)

ALLEGIANCE: Galactic Republic
FIRST APPEARANCE: THR: TB

As the medic on Master Volte's Pathfinder team, Grint Rupar is used to practicing healing far from civilization. He observes that it will take generations of work to extend the Republic communications network to the Outer Rim worlds.

PAKO

PRONOUNS: He/him
SPECIES: Nikto
HEIGHT: 1.75 m (5 ft 9 in)

ALLEGIANCE: Galactic Republic
FIRST APPEARANCE: THRA: TNT

Pako is the pilot on the Pathfinder ship *Witherbloom*, which collides with a Path ship that's transporting Nameless eggs. Inspired by his crewmate Ambar's ideas, Pako rigs the Path ship's engine to explode so it will kill the Nameless.

> "GREAT PLAN, PAKO. VOLUNTEER TO GO TO THE ENGINE ROOM ALONE."
>
> – Pako to himself

AMBAR

PRONOUNS: She/her
SPECIES: Mournish
HEIGHT: 1.65 m (5 ft 5 in)

ALLEGIANCE: Galactic Republic
FIRST APPEARANCE: THRA: TNT

Ambar is *Witherbloom*'s medic. As well as healing organic beings, she knows how to repair the team's EX communication droids. When her team and members of the Path of the Open Hand are attacked by the Nameless, Ambar comes up with a plan to electrify the hull of the Path's ship to repel the creatures.

KAM

PRONOUNS: He/him
SPECIES: Twi'lek
HEIGHT: 1.88 m (6 ft 2 in)

ALLEGIANCE: Galactic Republic
FIRST APPEARANCE: QftHC

Kam and fellow engineer Amos Tillian make up the communications team assigned to Jedi Master Silandra Sho's Republic Pathfinder mission. After receiving a message from an EX droid revealing that Jedi Master Rok Buran's Pathfinder team has run into trouble, Kam insists they contact Master Sho for help and head to the planet Aubadas.

"I DON'T THINK EVEN *IT* KNOWS WHAT IT'S TRYING TO SAY."

– Kam

AMOS TILLIAN

PRONOUNS: He/him
SPECIES: Theelin
HEIGHT: 1.70 m (5 ft 7 in)

ALLEGIANCE: Galactic Republic
FIRST APPEARANCE: QftHC

Amos Tillian and his colleague Kam develop a close working relationship after spending so much time together. On a mission to find a missing Pathfinder team on Aubadas, Amos and Kam work to reestablish communications. Amos grows impressed with the technology of Aubadas' local Katikoot population.

"WE COULD LEARN A LOT BY UNDERSTANDING THE KATIKOOT'S TECHNOLOGY."

– Amos Tillian

PRIV ITTIK

PRONOUNS: She/her
SPECIES: Iktotchi
HEIGHT: 1.75 m (5 ft 9 in)

ALLEGIANCE: Galactic Republic
FIRST APPEARANCE: Cat

Priv Ittik is a serious-minded Republic guard. She and fellow guard Lu Sweet accompany Jedi Creighton Sun and Aida Forte to Dalna as their security detail. Priv stays close to the Jedi and guards them in silence. She isn't thrilled when a Jedi youngling, Cippa Tarko, is added to their watch, though she is soon impressed by Cippa's bravery during battle.

"FROM HERE ON OUT, WE DON'T MOVE UNLESS MASTER YADDLE SAYS SO."

– Priv Ittik

LU SWEET

PRONOUNS: He/him
SPECIES: Human
HEIGHT: 1.85 m (6 ft 1 in)

ALLEGIANCE: Galactic Republic
FIRST APPEARANCE: Cat

According to Jedi Creighton Sun, Republic guard Lu Sweet looks like he is "spring-loaded for a fight." And when the time for fighting comes, during the Battle of Dalna, Lu is ready. He tries to fly the Jedi's ship in search of assistance, but the damaged ship crashes. Lu rejoins the Jedi and fights bravely, though he dies in battle.

"SHIELDS ARE DOWN. EVERYTHING IS DOWN. THIS SHIP IS TRASH."

– Lu Sweet

EX DROIDS

MESSAGE RELAYERS

- Wide view camera
- Reinforced radio antenna
- Mini thruster
- Retractable legs

TYPE: Communication droid
HEIGHT: (with legs extended) 97 cm (3 ft 2 in)

ALLEGIANCE: Galactic Republic
FIRST APPEARANCE: QftHC

EX communication droids are vital to the growth and exploration of the galaxy. Republic comms teams use EX droids to send messages. The droids are small but incredibly tough, often traveling alone through the far reaches of space to deliver information. They are often placed into thruster pods and rockets to fly at great speeds, and are designed not to burn up while entering or exiting atmospheres.

THE GREAT FRONTIER

EX droids are crucial in areas of the galaxy without communications buoys, or where the buoys have been hijacked or damaged. Jedi Master Rok Buran and his Pathfinder team send EX-8C out for help after they are attacked on Gloam. Kyong Greylark also uses EX droids to relay her message that she is stepping down as chancellor.

> "THEY'RE STURDY LITTLE THINGS, THESE EX MODELS. MOST DROIDS WOULDN'T HAVE MADE IT THIS FAR."
>
> – Amos Tillian

LINA SOH

SUPREME CHANCELLOR OF THE GALACTIC REPUBLIC

PRONOUNS: She/her
SPECIES: Human
HEIGHT: 1.70 m (5 ft 7 in)

ALLEGIANCE: Galactic Republic
FIRST APPEARANCE: LotJ

GREAT WORKS
Some of Soh's most ambitious projects include Starlight Beacon and the Republic Fair. Starlight Beacon, a space station run by a mix of Republic officials and Jedi, is the Republic's Outer Rim outpost. It sends out beacons that boost communications across the frontier and serves as a safe haven for those in need. The Republic Fair on the frontier planet Valo is intended to be a celebration of peace, unity, and hope—a symbol of the Republic's great achievements.

Lina's twin targons, Matari and Voru, are loyal only to her

The Galactic Republic's strongest champion, Lina Soh, puts all her time and energy into developing and protecting the Republic she was elected to serve. Soh is known for her "Great Works," a group of projects she set up in the hope of bringing more Outer Rim worlds into the embrace of the Republic. She has a close relationship with the Jedi Order. They work on various projects together, ranging from peace treaties to the installation of cross-galaxy communications relays.

Targons have four eyes and tufted tails

PERSONAL STRUGGLES

Not everyone in Soh's family is thrilled with her high-profile career. Her son, Kitrep, shies away from the spotlight and only begrudgingly attends the Republic Fair on Valo. Soh is aware that the Nihil remain a threat to the Republic, but she insists that the Fair proceed. She firmly believes it will be of immense benefit to the citizens of the Republic.

AFTERMATH

Soh is mistaken, and is gravely injured when the Nihil attack the Fair—but her immediate thoughts are not for herself. She fears for her son who is caught up in the attack, and she deeply regrets her arrogance for opening the Fair despite the Nihil threat. Soh commands the Republic Defense Coalition to muster a fleet against Marchion Ro. She wants the Republic's citizens to know they will not be abandoned during difficult times.

Robes chosen purposefully for each occasion

NIHIL THREAT

Soh's grand plans for the galaxy are threatened by the Great Disaster and the resulting dangers to hyperspace travel. She closes down many hyperspace lanes, a politically risky decision, but one she hopes will ensure the safety of Republic citizens. When the Nihil are discovered to be behind the catastrophe, Soh rallies the Republic and the Jedi to spare nothing in the effort to stop them.

"I WANT THESE NIHIL BROUGHT TO JUSTICE. EVERY LAST ONE."

– Lina Soh

STARLIGHT BEACON

One of the Great Works of Republic Chancellor Lina Soh, the space station Starlight Beacon is a shining example of what the Republic and Jedi can accomplish together. Built in the Outer Rim territories, where hyperspace travel and communications lines are still being developed, Starlight Beacon is the Republic's largest outreach effort to support the frontier. Starlight Beacon broadcasts a signal that can be heard far into the galaxy. The signal boosts existing communications lines and also serves as a welcome invitation to anyone in need.

COMMUNITY
Starlight Beacon is home to both Republic and Jedi staff. The space station has quarters for workers, visitors, and Jedi—some of whom are permanently stationed there. The docking bay welcomes ships from across the galaxy. A hospital, research tower, library, canteens, and meditation zones make Starlight Beacon a community of its own. Jedi Master Estala Maru and Republic officer Rodor Keen work together to run the day-to-day activities of the station. Their jobs are a never-ending challenge because every day on Starlight is different.

AID EFFORTS
Depending on the need of the time, Starlight is used as a meeting place for conferences, an evacuation location for Outer Rim worlds in danger, or as a base of operations for the Jedi in their fight against galactic threats. As a mobile base, it can even be towed to planets in distress to offer on-site aid.

After a volcanic catastrophe on Dalna, many ships tow Starlight to help in the rescue efforts there. Shortly after, Starlight flies over the planet Eiram to try to help a population under threat from massive cyclones.

THE FALL OF STARLIGHT

As a symbol of the combined strength of the Republic and the Jedi, Starlight Beacon becomes a target for those who wish to sow chaos in the galaxy. The Republic is betrayed by one of its own senators, Ghirra Starros, who steals schematics of the space station and hands them over to the Nihil. Nihil spies infiltrate the station and set off a bomb. The presence of Nameless creatures prevents the Jedi from being able to save the station, which breaks apart. As the Republic and Jedi reel from the loss of Starlight, Chancellor Lina Soh vows to not leave the Outer Rim territories in darkness.

GHAL TARPFEN

PRONOUNS: She/her
SPECIES: Mon Calamari
HEIGHT: 1.73 m (5 ft 8 in)

ALLEGIANCE: Galactic Republic, Mon Cala Royal Guard
FIRST APPEARANCE: SS: FD

Excellent underwater vision

Ghal Tarpfen is the no-nonsense head of security on Starlight Beacon. She always has security on her mind. Ghal interrogates a Nihil prisoner and gives her a light sentence hoping she will change her ways—though she doesn't realize the captive is Nihil Tempest Runner Lourna Dee. Later, the Nihil discover Ghal's prior relationship with the king of Mon Cala, so they try to blackmail her and then kidnap her. Ghal escapes long enough to send a message to Starlight, warning them of Nihil spies on board and in the Senate.

"EVERYONE DESERVES A SECOND CHANCE. IF THEY WANT ONE."

– Ghal Tarpfen

VELKO JAHEN

PRONOUNS: She/her
SPECIES: Soikan
HEIGHT: 1.68 m (5 ft 6 in)

ALLEGIANCE: Galactic Republic
FIRST APPEARANCE: SS: FD

Wanting a break from combat after serving in the Soikan Civil War, Velko Jahen joins the Republic administrative corps, where she is assigned to Starlight Beacon as an administrator and aide to head of operations, Rodor Keen. Velko isn't sure what to expect at first, but she soon becomes an important asset to Keen. Velko also develops good working relationships with other Starlight leaders, including Keen's Jedi counterpart, Estala Maru, and she is quick to act on her instincts when needed. With the help of Estala's droid, KC-78, Velko identifies an assassin who attempted to kill a Rion ambassador in Starlight's hospital.

"YOU'RE A LONG WAY FROM HOME, VEL."

– Velko Jahen to herself

RODOR KEEN

PRONOUNS: He/him
SPECIES: Human
HEIGHT: 1.78 m (5 ft 10 in)

ALLEGIANCE: Galactic Republic
FIRST APPEARANCE: THR (PI)

As head of operations on Starlight Beacon, Rodor Keen manages the space station along with Jedi Estala Maru. Both administrators are known for being hands-on, but Maru's sense of humor initially falls flat with the more serious-minded Rodor. It takes some time to establish a good working relationship.

GINO'LE

PRONOUNS: He/him
SPECIES: Anacondan
LENGTH: 4.70 m (15 ft 5 in)

ALLEGIANCE: Galactic Republic
FIRST APPEARANCE: SS: FD

As chief of medical operations, Anacondan doctor Gino'le oversees the hospital on Starlight Beacon. Gino'le cares for everyone, from visiting dignitaries to Jedi fighting off the effects of Drengir and Nameless attacks. He uses cybernetic limbs to help him with his day-to-day and medical tasks.

Anacondans have no limbs

PIKKA ADREN

PRONOUNS: She/her
SPECIES: Human
HEIGHT: 1.68 m (5 ft 6 in)

ALLEGIANCE: Galactic Republic
FIRST APPEARANCE: SS: GT

Pikka Adren never misses a single detail—in her favorite puzzles or at work—which makes her an excellent project manager to oversee the construction of Starlight Beacon alongside her husband, Joss. When Pikka notices an unexplained power surge in Starlight's system shortly before its opening ceremony, she is quick to postpone her vacation to fix the issue.

JOSS ADREN

PRONOUNS: He/him
SPECIES: Human
HEIGHT: 1.85 m (6 ft 1 in)

ALLEGIANCE: Galactic Republic
FIRST APPEARANCE: SS: GT

Joss Adren, along with his wife, Pikka, moves from constructing Starlight Beacon to fighting the Nihil at the Battle of Kur. Joss' excellent piloting skills, combined with Pikka's slicing expertise, help them counter the Nihil's mysterious hyperspace micro-jumps. Later, they both join a task force and set out to continue the hunt for the Nihil.

HEDDA CASSET

PRONOUNS: She/her
SPECIES: Human
HEIGHT: 1.68 m (5 ft 6 in)

ALLEGIANCE: Byne Guild
FIRST APPEARANCE: LotJ

Hedda Casset is the experienced captain of the *Legacy Run*. Transporting thousands of passengers, she is faced with a potential disaster—an obstacle in her hyperspace lane. Remaining calm and focused, Casset tries to steer the ship out of harm's way. The *Legacy Run* breaks apart but her quick, decisive actions save many passengers' lives.

SERJ UKKARIAN

PRONOUNS: He/him
SPECIES: Human
HEIGHT: 1.35 m (4 ft 5 in)

ALLEGIANCE: Unknown
FIRST APPEARANCE: LotJ

Serj Ukkarian is a passenger on the *Legacy Run*. He and the other children watch holos and play games during their long journey from the Core Worlds to the Outer Rim. When the *Legacy Run* breaks apart, Serj survives, but he worries that the disaster was caused by his slicing into the bridge systems, even though it was not.

"IT LOOKED LIKE THREE STRIKES OF LIGHTNING."

– Serj Ukkarian

PEVEL KRONARA

PRONOUNS: He/him
SPECIES: Human
HEIGHT: 1.75 m (5 ft 9 in)

ALLEGIANCE: Galactic Republic
FIRST APPEARANCE: SS: GT

Gruff military leader Pevel Kronara commands the *Third Horizon* cruiser, which is part of the Galactic Republic Defense Coalition. Kronara works closely with Republic Chancellor Lina Soh and Jedi Master Avar Kriss to help the people of Hetzal Prime after the Great Disaster, and to hunt down the Nihil at the Battle of Kur.

KEVEN TARR

PRONOUNS: He/him
SPECIES: Human
HEIGHT: 1.70 m (5 ft 7 in)

ALLEGIANCE: Hetzal Prime
FIRST APPEARANCE: LotJ

Brilliant but shy technician Keven Tarr creates an algorithm that uses droids to predict the locations where dangerous chunks of debris from the *Legacy Run* will drop out of hyperspace. His makeshift network protects his homeworld, Hetzal Prime, and a larger version goes on to help many other places in the galaxy. Tarr later takes a job with the San Tekka clan.

"I NEED DROIDS. I NEED A LOT."

– Keven Tarr

TIA TOON

PRONOUNS: He/him
SPECIES: Sullustan
HEIGHT: 1.35 m (4 ft 5 in)

ALLEGIANCE: Galactic Republic
FIRST APPEARANCE: TRS

Senator Tia Toon represents Sullust in the Galactic Senate. Toon believes the Republic relies too much on the Jedi as their protectors, so he is in favor of the Defense Force Program, a military operation that is run and managed by the Republic.

IZZET NOOR

PRONOUNS: He/him
SPECIES: Human
HEIGHT: 1.78 m (5 ft 10 in)

ALLEGIANCE: Galactic Republic
FIRST APPEARANCE: LotJ

Izzet Noor serves as the senator for Serenno. Speaking on behalf of the majority of the Outer Rim territories, Noor expresses his alarm over the hyperspace closures ordered by Chancellor Lina Soh after the Great Disaster. Unbeknownst to Noor, his aide, Jeni Wataro, is secretly working for the Nihil.

KITREP SOH

PRONOUNS: He/him
SPECIES: Human
HEIGHT: 1.68 m (5 ft 6 in)

ALLEGIANCE: Galactic Republic
FIRST APPEARANCE: TRS

Kitrep Soh is the son of Lina Soh, the Supreme Chancellor of the Republic. He accompanies his mother to the Republic Fair on Valo even though he would rather avoid crowds and keep out of the spotlight. Kitrep and Jom Lariin, son of the mayor of Lonisa City on Valo, sneak off from the Fair just before the Nihil attack. After his mother is gravely injured, Soh stays by her side while she recovers.

CEERIL

PRONOUNS: He/him
SPECIES: Skembo
HEIGHT: 91 cm (3 ft)

ALLEGIANCE: Rion government
FIRST APPEARANCE: SS: FD

Injured by *Legacy Run* debris following the Great Disaster, Ceeril, an ambassador from the planet Rion, seeks refuge in Starlight Beacon's hospital. After annoying Starlight staff with his never-ending commands and complaints, Ceeril attempts to frame a Hassarian (a rival species to Skembos) for an assassination attempt against his life.

"WHAT IS THE MEANING OF THIS?"

– Ceeril

CHAPTER FOUR

CITIZENS

Space travelers can expect to meet all sorts of citizens on their adventures, from royalty, mercenaries, and pilots to bartenders, Force users, and pirates.

FORCE HUB

The Holy City on Jedha attracts a large number of Force-worshipping groups and is home to the Convocation of the Force, an organization that connects Force sects, each with their own Force philosophies. The local Enlightenment bar caters to an always evolving mix of travelers and pilgrims.

NEW PATHS THROUGH SPACE

In this time of growth, hyperspace prospecting is a popular, yet risky, way to make a fortune. Prospectors map and sell hyperspace paths as a living. Buyers can make the routes public, though some keep them secret, using them to gain advantage over others.

RULE MAKERS AND RULE BREAKERS

From the Core Worlds to the Unknown Regions, pirates, outlaws, and criminals cause chaos while Republic patrols, lawmakers, and Jedi strive to keep order. Some groups loom larger than others, but citizens everywhere remain the constant heartbeat of an ever-changing galaxy.

CONVOCATION OF THE FORCE

Jedha is home to many groups that worship the Force in some way. The Convocation of the Force is an organization that aims to generate peace and understanding between different Force sects. The Convocation includes representatives from various groups, all of which have different histories and beliefs about the power and meaning of the Force. While the goal of the Convocation is to bring diverse groups together, it has also become a target for those who see the Force—and Force users—as a threat.

JEDI ORDER

The Jedi believe that the Force is an energy field created by all living things that binds the galaxy together and gives them their power. The Jedi stay true to the light side of the Force, strong in their belief that anger, hate, and fear are paths to the dark side.

GUARDIANS OF THE WHILLS

The Guardians of the Whills, who strive to be one with the Force, are one of the oldest groups on Jedha. Guardians protect the Temple of the Kyber, the ancient artifacts that are stored there, and the many pilgrims who have traveled from afar to visit the temple.

Sorcerers of Tund

Jedi

Jedi

Lonto

Matukai

MATUKAI

The Matukai are a sect who see themselves as defenders of the light side of the Force. Their philosophy leads many of them to have extremely negative opinions of groups associated with the dark side, such as the Yacombe, who they believe are dark-side worshippers.

SORCERERS OF TUND

The Sorcerers of Tund are a group of mystics associated with the dark side of the Force. They refer to the Force as "the Unity."

LONTO

The Lonto are light-side Force users with a special connection to nature. Through a mystical power they use vines, plants, and leaves to protect and heal others.

DISCIPLES OF THE WHILLS

Disciples of the Whills, customarily seen wearing red robes, seek to understand the will of the Force through meditation. As such, they do not shun the dark side as they believe that it and the light side must always remain in balance.

FALLANASSI

The Fallanassi refer to the light side of the Force as the "white current" and the dark side of the Force as the "dark tide." They train to use the light side of the Force, and are adept at projecting illusions of themselves to other parts of the galaxy.

CHURCH OF THE FORCE

Members of the Church of the Force are not Force-sensitive, but they choose to follow many of the same teachings as the Jedi Order. Along with the Disciples and Guardians of the Whills, Church of the Force members honor the Temple of the Kyber as a holy site.

Jedi

Church of the Force

Jedi

Disciples of the Whills

TARNA MIAK

SORCERER OF TUND

Ceremonial headpiece made from metal mined on Tund

Sorcerers of Tund cover most of their body with wrappings

PRONOUNS: He/him
SPECIES: Human
HEIGHT: 1.68 m (5 ft 6 in)

ALLEGIANCE: Sorcerers of Tund, Convocation of the Force
FIRST APPEARANCE: THR (PII)

Tarna Miak represents the Sorcerers of Tund—a Force sect with ties to the dark side—at the Convocation of the Force. When the Path of the Open Hand unleashes a Nameless, Tarna is one of the first to feel the effects. Seeing monsters in every face in the crowd, Tarna unleashes his power until Jedi Master Vildar Mac is able to snap him out of his visions.

SORCERER OF OLD

During the Battle of Jedha, Tarna shelters in the Enlightenment bar together with Vildar and his Padawan, Matthea Cathley. After hearing Vildar's childhood memory of a scary cloaked figure, Tarna explains that it was an outcast from the Sorcerers of Tund, expelled for embracing the dark side.

"THE LAST THING I EXPECTED WAS TO FIND A JEDI IN THE MIDDLE OF A COMMON BRAWL."

– Tarna Miak to Vildar Mac

TEY SIRREK

SEPHI TRICKSTER

Spherical droid SK-0T, or "Skoot," follows Tey, recording everything around them

Cloak provides quick cover in crowds

Lightbow is the traditional weapon of the Guardians of the Whills

PRONOUNS: He/him
SPECIES: Sephi
HEIGHT: 1.85 m (6 ft 1 in)

ALLEGIANCE: None
FIRST APPEARANCE: THR (PII)

Tey Sirrek is a former Guardian of the Whills who lives in the Holy City on Jedha. Many of the locals believe him to be a nuisance or a criminal. Still, he tries his best to help people in need, especially those who have no one else to turn to. Tey can produce a pheromone that renders living things unconscious.

"YOU DON'T WANT TO DO THIS,
 BIG MAN. TRUST ME, I KNOW.
 YOU'RE BETTER THAN THIS."

– Tey Sirrek to Vildar Mac

TWO MAKES A TEAM

Tey is unpredictable and eccentric, which are not qualities Jedi Master Vildar Mac initially appreciates when the two cross paths on Jedha. But Vildar quickly sees past Tey's dubious reputation and the two form a strong friendship. Tey uses a Sith gauntlet—the Hand of Siberus—to try to protect Vildar when he is overcome by a Nameless creature, and later helps pull the Jedi Master away from the dark side.

SIRENÉ

PRONOUNS: She/her
SPECIES: Human
HEIGHT: 1.63 m (5 ft 4 in)

ALLEGIANCE: Fallanassi, Convocation of the Force
FIRST APPEARANCE: THR (PII)

Sirené is the Fallanassi representative to the Convocation of the Force on Jedha. Fallanassi embrace only the light side of the Force, which they refer to as the "white current." Sirené is upset when a delegate from another Force group, the Yacombe, petitions to join the Convocation, since she believes the Yacombe are aligned with the dark side of the Force. Sirené draws her two blades against the Yacombe envoy, but stops her attack at the urging of Jedi Knight Oliviah Zeveron.

"THE FALLANASSI
FOLLOW THE WHITE
CURRENT ALONE."

– Sirené

YACOMBE DELEGATE

PRONOUNS: She/her
SPECIES: Unknown
HEIGHT: 1.65 m (5 ft 5 in)

ALLEGIANCE: Yacombe
FIRST APPEARANCE: THR (PII)

Violence erupts when an envoy from the Yacombe, a group once aligned with the dark side of the Force, applies to join the Convocation of the Force. The Yacombe people do not speak directly, so a Ximpi proxy speaks for the delegate instead. The proxy argues that the Yacombe broke with the dark side many years ago and are now neutral, favoring neither the light nor the dark side. However, many Convocation representatives doubt the Yacombe's intentions and speak out strongly against them. After a series of tense exchanges and angry outbursts, the delegate rescinds her application.

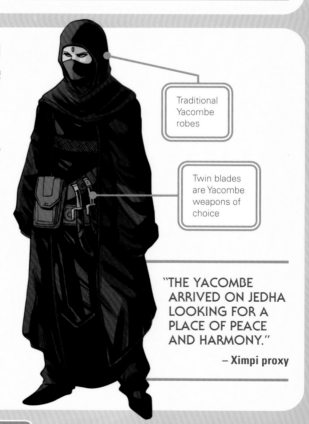

Traditional Yacombe robes

Twin blades are Yacombe weapons of choice

"THE YACOMBE
ARRIVED ON JEDHA
LOOKING FOR A
PLACE OF PEACE
AND HARMONY."

– Ximpi proxy

KILAN T'DARA

PRONOUNS: She/her
SPECIES: Ayrou
HEIGHT: 1.60 m (5 ft 3 in)

ALLEGIANCE: Church of the Force, Convocation of the Force
FIRST APPEARANCE: THR (PII)

Kilan T'Dara is the representative for the Church of the Force as well as the chair of the advisory council for Force-related groups, the Convocation of the Force. Like all Church of the Force members, Kilan is not Force-sensitive, but follows the beliefs of the Jedi Order. As the Convocation's leader, Kilan must remain as neutral as possible during disputes between member groups of the Convocation. Her desire to keep the peace sometimes puts her at odds with being honest to those outside the Convocation.

Aurodium necklace

"IT IS FOR THE GOOD OF THE PEOPLE."

– Kilan T'Dara

ELRIS FLORENT

PRONOUNS: She/her
SPECIES: Unknown
HEIGHT: 1.73 m (5 ft 8 in)

ALLEGIANCE: Disciple of the Whills, Convocation of the Force
FIRST APPEARANCE: THR (PII)

Elris Florent is a Disciple of the Whills, one of the oldest Force-worshipping groups on Jedha. She listens for the will of the Force and works closely with the Guardians of the Whills, who protect the Temple of the Kyber. Elris represents the Disciples of the Whills within the Convocation of the Force. When the Yacombe, another group of Force users, apply to join the Convocation, Elris remains calm and open to hearing their side, even while other Convocation members threaten violence.

Symbol represents the will of the Force

"I KNOW WE SHOULD LISTEN TO THEIR APPLICATION. WE OWE THEM THAT AT LEAST."

– Elris Florent

WARAN VAL

PRONOUNS: He/him
SPECIES: Kel Dor
HEIGHT: 1.45 m (4 ft 9 in)

ALLEGIANCE: Matukai, Convocation of the Force
FIRST APPEARANCE: THR (PII)

Traditional wan-shen have a blade on one end and are used for close combat

Waran Val is the Matukai representative to the Convocation of the Force on Jedha. Naturally suspicious, Val is quick to anger when he feels threatened. He is a master of the martial arts and raises his wan-shen in defense of the light side of the Force during a Convocation hearing. Later, when the Herald of the Path of the Open Hand proposes the Convocation disband, Val voices his strong opposition. He argues that the Matukai, as well as the Lonto people, do not in any way abuse their use of the Force.

"THE MATUKAI RESPECT THE FORCE IN ALL MATTERS."

– Waran Val

SUSALEE

PRONOUNS: She/her
SPECIES: Lonto
HEIGHT: 1.85 m (6 ft 1 in)

ALLEGIANCE: Convocation of the Force
FIRST APPEARANCE: THR (PII)

Susalee is the Lonto representative to the Convocation of the Force. The Lonto worship the light side of the Force and are proud to have a special connection with nature. Susalee's Force powers allow her to use vines and leaves as weapons or healing aids. After a bombing at the Temple of the Kyber, she uses tragia leaves to help heal the wounds of Jedi Master Vildar Mac. Susalee later loses control and unleashes her vines into the crowd on the steps of the Convocation when she is affected by the presence of a Nameless creature.

"WE CHANNEL ITS POWER, BUT ONLY FOR THE GOOD OF THE NATURAL WORLD."

– Susalee

OKLANE VISS

PRONOUNS: He/him
SPECIES: Falleen
HEIGHT: 1.60 m (5 ft 3 in)

ALLEGIANCE: Guardians of the Whills
FIRST APPEARANCE: THR (PII)

Oklane Viss is the hard-nosed captain of the Guardians of the Whills on Jedha. He takes his role as protector of the relics stored in the Temple of the Kyber very seriously and does not have patience for anyone who questions his methods. Viss believes that Guardians need to keep their focus entirely on protecting the temple, and that they do not need to concern themselves with the crimes—or anything else—happening in the city. This puts him at odds with former Guardian Tey Sirrek, who wants to help anyone in need on Jedha.

"IT IS NOT YOU THAT WE HAVE A PROBLEM WITH, JEDI—IT'S THAT TRAITOR."

– Oklane Viss about Tey Sirrek

MYTION

PRONOUNS: He/him
SPECIES: Human
HEIGHT: 1.75 m (5 ft 9 in)

ALLEGIANCE: Brothers of the Ninth Door
FIRST APPEARANCE: TBoJ

Mytion is a member of the Brothers of the Ninth Door, a group who wear bone masks some believe are made from the skulls of their own dead. The Brothers have the ability to cloud people's minds to hide their appearance. They are not part of the Convocation of the Force, and they don't preach like the Path of the Open Hand, preferring to keep a lower profile. Mytion makes a deal with prospector Tilson Graf to bomb the Eiram–E'ronoh ceasefire signing, hoping his sect will win public favor after helping to rebuild the city.

"I SHALL BUILD A NEW LODGE FOR MY ORDER… A NEW PLACE OF WORSHIP AMONGST THE CHURCHES AND TEMPLES OF THE OTHER RELIGIONS… THE BROTHERS WILL BE ON HAND TO ASSIST IN THE REBUILDING. WE SHALL EARN THE RESPECT OF THE PEOPLE AND BE DULY RECOGNIZED AND ACCEPTED BY THE CONVOCATION."

– Mytion, about the Brothers of the Ninth Door

MAZ KANATA

PIRATE QUEEN

Goggles include lenses of varying strengths

Buckle includes secret compartment

PRONOUNS: She/her
SPECIES: Unknown
HEIGHT: 1.25 m (4 ft 1 in)

ALLEGIANCE: Maz's crew
FIRST APPEARANCE:
THRA (PI)

Perceptive and wise, Maz Kanata is not a Jedi—though she is Force-sensitive. Maz has gained the respect of scoundrels, smugglers, and Jedi over the course of her long life. Based on the Mid Rim planet Takodana, Maz welcomes everyone to her castle, where she runs a crew that includes hyperspace prospector Dexter Jettster and undercover Padawan Sav Malagán.

FAITHFUL CREW

Maz's crew use her ship, the *Venomed Scabbard*, on many missions, and Maz counts on a Hoover named Abadoo to keep the ship running. While investigating the Dank Graks criminal gang, Maz is abducted. Her crew swiftly set out to find her. Maz inspires loyalty from her crewmates, allies, and acquaintances. Her friendship with Sav Malagán lasts more than 100 years.

"GEAR UP FOR MAXIMUM CHAOS!"

– Maz Kanata

DEXTER JETTSTER

RENOWNED HYPERSPACE PROSPECTOR

PRONOUNS: He/him
SPECIES: Besalisk
HEIGHT: 1.88 m (6 ft 2 in)

ALLEGIANCE: Maz's crew
FIRST APPEARANCE:
THRA (PII)

Dexter Jettster is an excellent hyperspace prospector, and an even better storyteller. He loves being the center of attention in a noisy crowd. An excellent judge of character, Dexter is very perceptive of his surroundings, a skill that comes in handy while charting new hyperspace paths in the rough, and often dangerous, frontier.

CREW LOYALTY

Dexter has a close relationship with Maz Kanata but he agrees to keep Sav Malagán's secret—that she is Force-sensitive—realizing that Sav might become an important ally.

After Maz is kidnapped by the Dank Graks, Dexter leads the rest of Maz's crew to find her. They follow the Graks to Jedha, which is under siege from the Path of the Open Hand.

Traveling cloak can conceal Dexter's four arms

Pockets store maps and trinkets

"COME ON, KID, WE GOTTA TELL MAZ WHAT WE HEARD."

— Dexter Jettster to Sav Malagán

ALAK

PRONOUNS: He/him
SPECIES: Human cyborg
HEIGHT: 2.26 m (7 ft 5 in)

ALLEGIANCE: Maz's crew
FIRST APPEARANCE: THRA (PII)

Alak is a gruff pirate who associates with Maz Kanata's crew of smugglers and outlaws on Takodana. He is hard to miss because his head and torso are covered in tattoos, while the lower part of his body has been replaced with cybernetic spider legs. According to legend, Alak once took over a battle station unassisted and saved a planet from invaders. Wanted in many systems, Alak has a complicated relationship with pirate hunter Inspector Raf, which he enjoys talking about.

Alak's droid T-8T

QUIET SHAN

PRONOUNS: She/her
SPECIES: Human cyborg
HEIGHT: 1.73 m (5 ft 8 in)

ALLEGIANCE: Maz's crew
FIRST APPEARANCE: THRA (PII)

Quiet Shan is part of Maz Kanata's pirate crew and the protégé of tattooed outlaw Alak. Shan rarely speaks, and it's rumored that when she does trouble is soon to follow. Nobody knows the story behind Shan's helmet, which covers half her face. Rumor has it the last person who asked her about it didn't survive the conversation. Suspicious of outsiders and a bit moody compared to her rambunctious fellow pirates, Quiet Shan can always be counted on by her peers during missions.

Helmet made from a nyix-alloy

Gold vambrace protects an old wound

Torso armor includes one huge sheet of metal

Officer Rado rides on Vizzle's back or torso

COROMONT VIZZLE

PRONOUNS: He/him
SPECIES: Unknown
HEIGHT: 1.85 m (6 ft 1 in)
ALLEGIANCE: Maz's crew

FIRST APPEARANCE:
THRA (PII)

Coromont Vizzle is a cheerful, sociable criminal who aligns himself with Maz Kanata's crew of pirates. He can regularly be heard singing songs (which he wrote himself) about his past exploits. Vizzle is arrested so frequently that a court insists an officer should accompany him wherever he goes—which is why Vizzle and the small Officer Rado can regularly be found arguing about the legality of whatever situation Vizzle has gotten himself into.

THERM SCISSORPUNCH

PRONOUNS: He/him
SPECIES: Nephran
HEIGHT: 1.96 m (6 ft 5 in)
ALLEGIANCE: Maz's crew

FIRST APPEARANCE:
THRA (PII)

Therm Scissorpunch is quick to brag about his pirating escapades. While many people doubt the truth of some of his stories, his large, powerful claw hands convince most to take him at his word. Scissorpunch spends most of his time at Maz Kanata's castle on Takodana, where he joins a card game or two or heads out with Maz and her crew on various missions.

Nephrans can live for hundreds of years

Claw conceals hidden blade

RADICAZ "SUNSHINE" DOBBS

OPPORTUNISTIC HYPERSPACE PROSPECTOR

Helmet includes built-in flashlight

Dobbs is quick to use his blaster against rivals

PRONOUNS: He/him
SPECIES: Human
HEIGHT: 1.70 m (5 ft 7 in)

ALLEGIANCE: None
FIRST APPEARANCE: PoD

Radicaz "Sunshine" Dobbs is a hyperspace prospector known for his navigation skills and his love of gambling. From his ship, the *Scupper*, he collects and sells ancient artifacts to the highest bidder. Dobbs' desire for fortune leads him to betray fellow prospector Spence Leffbruk after they team up to find a route to the mysterious Planet X.

DEADLY GIFT

Dobbs gives the Mother—the leader of the Path of the Open Hand—what he believes to be a jewel strong with the Force. However, it is actually an egg that hatches a creature known as a Nameless, which can overwhelm and kill Force users. Enchanted by the Mother, Dobbs agrees to help her in any way he can.

He accompanies Path members to Jedha to help them steal more Force-related artifacts, and also returns to Planet X to collect more Nameless eggs for the Mother.

"WHAT DOESN'T KILL US ONLY MAKES US RICHER."

– Radicaz "Sunshine" Dobbs

SPENCE LEFFBRUK

PRONOUNS: He/him
SPECIES: Human
HEIGHT: 1.73 m (5 ft 8 in)

ALLEGIANCE: None
FIRST APPEARANCE: QftHC

Hyperspace prospector Spence Leffbruk lives to explore new worlds and meet new people. Along with his son, Dass, Leffbruk charts routes in the Outer Rim, never slowed by an old arm injury that serves as a reminder of the accident that killed his wife. Leffbruk makes a deal with fellow prospector Radicaz "Sunshine" Dobbs when they are both heading to the same mysterious planet. But Dobbs betrays both father and son, abandoning them on the monster-ridden planet Gloam. Still, Leffbruk retains his sense of humor as he and his son struggle to survive.

Pockets full of trinkets he collects along the way

"I MADE A PROMISE TO YOUR MOTHER THAT I'D LOOK AFTER YOU."

– Spence Leffbruk to Dass

KATIKOOT

SPECIES: Katikoot
HEIGHT: 2.44 m (8 ft)

ALLEGIANCE: Katikoot
FIRST APPEARANCE: QftHC

The Katikoot people live on the planet Aubadas under the leadership of Kittik. Kittik's daughter, Mittik, helps Jedi Rooper Nitani and Silandra Sho search for a missing Jedi on the nearby planet Gloam. While there, Mittik discovers that her people originated on Gloam. She works to recover what little mineral fuel remains in the mines there to add to her people's failing energy reserves. But Mittik's cousin Rillik betrays his fellow miners, unleashing monsters from the depths of the mines. He plans for the monsters to destroy all witnesses, leaving him free to sell the fuel.

"THE KATIKOOT WILL SEE TO THEIR OWN PROBLEMS FROM NOW ON."

– Mittik

DASS LEFFBRUK

NOVICE HYPERSPACE PROSPECTOR

Macrobinoculars

Tactical hiking stick

Utility hat provides shade

PRONOUNS: He/him
SPECIES: Human
HEIGHT: 1.55 m (5 ft 1 in)

ALLEGIANCE: None
FIRST APPEARANCE: QftHC

Dass Leffbruk has spent his entire life traveling the galaxy with his father, Spence, as a hyperspace prospector-in-training. Secretly, Dass dreams of becoming a Pathfinder but he worries his father will not approve. Dass can be shy at times, but he finds courage when he and his father are betrayed by another prospector, "Sunshine" Dobbs.

FINDING HIS OWN WAY

After Dobbs' betrayal, Dass decides he needs to set things right. Instead of joining his father's crew for the Hyperspace Chase, Dass teams up with new friends, Padawan Rooper Nitani and pilot Sky Graf. He intends to make his way to the mysterious Planet X, where he hopes to retrieve his father's lost ship and the only holo he has of his mother.

"SPACE FLIGHT IS ALWAYS DANGEROUS. ESPECIALLY PROSPECTING. I'M READY!"

– Dass Leffbruk

SKY GRAF

AMBITIOUS HYPERSPACE PROSPECTOR

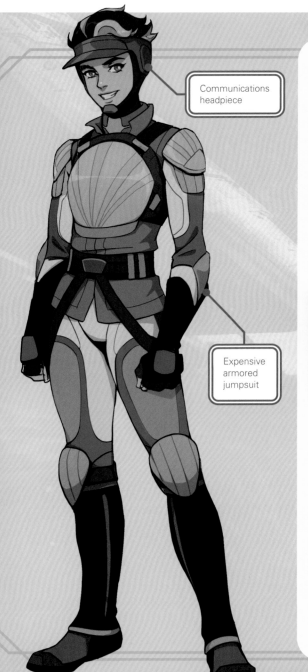

Communications headpiece

Expensive armored jumpsuit

PRONOUNS: They/them
SPECIES: Human
HEIGHT: 1.57 m (5 ft 2 in)

ALLEGIANCE: Graf family
FIRST APPEARANCE: QfPX

Confident, talented, and a little bit reckless, Sky Graf strives to prove their worth to their powerful hyperspace prospecting clan. Feeling pressure to add to their family's fame and fortune, Sky can come off as brash and selfish. But Sky's desire to chart a course to Planet X is also driven by their hope to find Sky's missing father, who is presumed dead after disappearing during a mission there.

CHANGING PRIORITIES

As a Graf, Sky is used to getting what they want without compromise. Initially, Sky is laser-focused on finding their father, but they agree to take a detour to the planet Dalna to help reunite Padawan Rooper Nitani with her master. Sky fixes Dalna's communications buoys, which have been sabotaged by the Path of the Open Hand.

"MOST PEOPLE DON'T BELIEVE PLANET X EXISTS, AND IF THEY DO, THEY DON'T THINK THAT THE SEARCH IS WORTH THE EFFORT."

– Sky Graf

ENLIGHTENMENT BAR

BAR SCENE

Visitors to Enlightenment will first notice the big, red double doors marked with the bar's name. Guarding them are the Twinkle Sisters, a pair of hulking Gloovan bodyguards ready to toss out anyone who gets too rowdy. At the bar sit regulars such as Moona, Piralli, and Keth Cerapath, loosening their tongues with goblets of retsa or blue mappa. The Iktotchi musician Madelina plays the electro-harp in the background, producing music that some find soothing even though it sounds like a strange, looping noise. Visitors are likely to hear tall tales of derring-do rising above the babble of voices, music, and laughter.

ALL OPINIONS WELCOME

Enlightenment's doors are open to any being of any creed—light side, dark side, or something entirely different. For that reason, energetic but (usually) friendly debates abound on the nature of the Force and the universe. Conversations are generally loud and raucous here, in contrast to the

Patrons may not find the spiritual enlightenment the name claims, yet Jedha's Enlightenment bar is a place where people from various Force sects can mingle peacefully. Owner Kradon Minst often joins his regular bartender, Chantho, at the counter to serve drinks. Kradon makes the most of his diverse mix of visitors to ply his trade as an information broker, selling or trading gossip and chatter. Many beings who have business on Jedha or nearby find themselves in Enlightenment—from mysterious Force worshippers and dusty droids to hyperspace prospectors and Jedi.

hushed, reverent tones used in the local houses of worship. However, the exchange of ideas in Enlightenment is still faithful—worshippers of different sects usually wish each other well before going back out into the world with their separate beliefs.

BACK DOOR

During the Battle of Jedha, the bar comes under siege. Kradon keeps business going even while people shelter from the riot outside. The crowd eventually breaks into the bar, shattering its back doors. However, Kradon has installed energy fields that can shield the bar even if its physical walls are knocked down. Wily Kradon also hides the fact that a hidden trapdoor leads to an old smugglers' tunnel, dug back in the days when the Jedi had a stronger presence on Jedha. It stretches all the way to the desert outside the city. The passageway is falling apart and infested with vermin, but it's still a way out in a pinch.

KRADON MINST

PROPRIETOR OF ENLIGHTENMENT

Protective shell carapace

Mixes drinks for many different species

Desert glass retsa goblet

PRONOUNS: He/him
SPECIES: Villarandi
HEIGHT: 1.22 m (4 ft)

ALLEGIANCE: Enlightenment bar
FIRST APPEARANCE: ToE: NP

Kradon Minst owns the Enlightenment bar on Jedha. It is a place where beings of any creed or species can stop for a drink. Kradon prides himself on being a source of useful information, which he gleans by listening for gossip and secrets. Neither the information nor the drinks come for free—unless it's for a regular for whom he has a soft spot, like Keth Cerapath.

"ALL ARE WELCOME IN ENLIGHTENMENT...
 PROVIDED THEY PAY THEIR BILLS."

– Kradon Minst

DEALINGS WITH THE JEDI

Kradon employs two intimidating bouncers known as the Twinkle Sisters to watch the bar's front door. He doesn't trust Jedi, believing that a lightsaber is more likely to be used against him than to help him. However, that doesn't prevent him from welcoming Jedi to the bar. Kradon gives Keth Cerapath and Jedi Silandra Sho the information they need on a mission, and during the Battle of Jedha he also helps Tey Sirrek, Vildar Mac, and Matty Cathley escape the city.

KETH CERAPATH

PRONOUNS: He/him
SPECIES: Human
HEIGHT: 1.73 m (5ft 8 in)

ALLEGIANCE: Jedi,
Enlightenment bar
FIRST APPEARANCE: ToE: NP

Temple of the Kyber worker Keth Cerapath spends his days sweeping the temple floors or hanging out at the Enlightenment bar. Keth is tired of his day-to-day life, and dreams of an adventure that will help him make a name for himself. His wish comes true when he accompanies Republic official Morton San Tekka to the ceasefire talks between warring planets Eiram and E'ronoh. But when Morton dies in an explosion and the treaty descends into chaos, Keth joins Jedi Silandra Sho to find the culprits. He goes on to help survivors reach shelter, but tragically dies protecting Silandra.

"ALL I WANT IS A BIT OF EXCITEMENT."

– Keth Cerapath

TWINKLE SISTERS

PRONOUNS: Both: She/her
SPECIES: Gloovan
HEIGHT: 2.29 m (7 ft 6 in)

ALLEGIANCE: Enlightenment
bar
FIRST APPEARANCE: ToE: NP

The Twinkle Sisters, Camille and Delphine, are the bouncers at the Enlightenment bar. They make sure no one gets too rowdy or leaves without paying. When rioters break into the bar during the Battle of Jedha, the Twinkle Sisters push the crowd back with stun bolts from their blasters. They protect Jedi Vildar Mac and Matty Cathley and their local friend Tey Sirrek, who are driven into the bar by the angry crowd. Despite the fact that no one except bar owner Kradon and a few privileged others are supposed to know about it, Camille reveals the existence of a secret escape route in Enlightenment's floor.

P3-7A

PRONOUNS: He/him
TYPE: Church droid
HEIGHT: 1.52 m (5 ft)

ALLEGIANCE: Keth Cerapath
FIRST APPEARANCE: TBoJ

P3-7A is the droid companion of Jedha local Keth Cerapath. Once abandoned and sold for scrap, he was rebuilt by a group of Bonbraks. P3-7A's vocoder used to belong to a Church of the Force droid, so he speaks entirely in quotations from holy texts.

"BLESSED ARE THOSE WHO WALK THE PATH OF LIGHT."

– P3-7A

JINX PICKWICK

PRONOUNS: She/her
SPECIES: Human
HEIGHT: 1.68 m (5 ft 6 in)

ALLEGIANCE: Dalna
FIRST APPEARANCE: PoD

Jinx Pickwick is the no-nonsense sheriff who protects the basin area that surrounds the town of Ferdan on Dalna. Ferdan is the closest town to the Path of the Open Hand compound. When Jinx learns of a flood warning, she tells Path member Marda Ro and her Jedi friend, Kevmo Zink, that heavy rains are coming.

"I WAS ELECTED TO KEEP EVERYONE HERE IN THE BASIN SAFE."

– Jinx Pickwick

PIRALLI

PRONOUNS: He/him
SPECIES: Sullustan
HEIGHT: 1.52 m (5 ft)

ALLEGIANCE: None
FIRST APPEARANCE: ToE: NP

Piralli is a Jedha dock worker, often found with his friend Moona at the Enlightenment bar bantering over refreshments and arguing about silly ideas. Piralli often mocks fellow bar regular Keth Cerapath for putting up with his droid P3-7A's quirks. Piralli enjoys partying with his friends, but he tends to see the negative side of things and sometimes gets into fights with other Jedha locals.

"'NOTHER ROUND?"

– Piralli

MOONA

PRONOUNS: She/her
SPECIES: Twi'lek
HEIGHT: 1.80 m (5 ft 11 in)

ALLEGIANCE: None
FIRST APPEARANCE: ToE: NP

Moona is a former pirate and a regular at the Enlightenment bar on Jedha. She can often be spotted with dock worker Piralli, cynically discussing other patrons or complaining about everything, from the crowds at the Festival of Balance to Keth Cerapath being late for their usual chat. After the Battle of Jedha, Moona buys a drink for Jedi Silandra Sho.

"AS IF I HAVE ANYWHERE ELSE TO BE."

– Moona

HELIS GRAF

PRONOUNS: He/him
ALLEGIANCE: Graf family
SPECIES: Human
FIRST APPEARANCE: QfPX
HEIGHT: 1.75 m (5 ft 9 in)

Helis Graf is Sky Graf's older brother and the owner of the ship the *Brightbird*. While Helis is busy organizing the Hyperspace Chase, Sky steals the *Brightbird* to search for Planet X. Helis pursues Sky and slices into the ship's controls to try to get it back. While Helis is angry with his younger sibling, he is also concerned that Sky comes to no harm.

"I WON'T LET UP, SKY. THAT'S MY SHIP.
   THIS IS MY RACE."

— Helis Graf

TILSON GRAF

PRONOUNS: He/him
ALLEGIANCE: Graf family
SPECIES: Human
FIRST APPEARANCE: TBoJ
HEIGHT: 1.70 m (5 ft 7 in)

Graf family outcast Tilson Graf arrives on Jedha claiming a desire to witness the historic signing of the Eiram–E'ronoh peace treaty. But Tilson is no mere bystander. He orchestrates a deadly bombing that disrupts the signing, then seeks out his secret partner—the Mother of the Path of the Open Hand.

"WE BOTH KNOW IT DOESN'T PAY TO
   LEAVE LOOSE ENDS AROUND."

— Tilson Graf

MORTON SAN TEKKA

PRONOUNS: He/him
ALLEGIANCE: San Tekka clan
SPECIES: Human
FIRST APPEARANCE: TBoJ
HEIGHT: 1.73 m (5 ft 8 in)

Morton San Tekka is asked to be the neutral official who oversees the peace treaty signing between Eiram and E'ronoh. His role is largely ceremonial, but Morton enlists the help of a local, Keth Cerapath, to ensure it all goes well. Unfortunately, the event is bombed and Morton loses his life.

"IT'S QUITE AN HONOR FOR A SAN TEKKA
   TO BE CHOSEN TO OVERSEE
   SUCH A KEY MATTER."

— Morton San Tekka

RIC FARAZI

PRONOUNS: She/her
ALLEGIANCE: None
SPECIES: Zeltron
FIRST APPEARANCE: PoV
HEIGHT: 1.75 m (5 ft 9 in)

Journalist Ric Farazi is investigating a rumored criminal operation on Dalna. Her questions lead her to the Path of the Open Hand. While Farazi sees Path members as true believers, she wonders if the Mother might be linked to reports of missing relics and weapons.

"THE PATH MEMBERS SAID SHE CAME TO
   THEM OUT OF THE BLUE, CLAIMING
   TO HAVE VISIONS OF THE FORCE."

— Ric Farazi, about the Mother

AXEL GREYLARK

CORUSCANT SCOUNDREL

Ornate epaulet

Shimmersilk thread details

PRONOUNS: He/him
SPECIES: Human
HEIGHT: 1.78 m (5 ft 10 in)

ALLEGIANCE: Galactic Republic, Path of the Open Hand
FIRST APPEARANCE: Con

Clever and charming, Axel Greylark has a reputation as a privileged party boy. He feels suffocated as Chancellor Kyong Greylark's son, and has never truly dealt with the pain of his father's death. Axel's desire to rebel and find belonging makes him an excellent target for the Mother as she looks to recruit new members to the Path of the Open Hand.

CHASING REDEMPTION
Axel blames the Jedi for his father's death, but he is immediately impressed when he meets Jedi Gella Nattai. Though he is ordered by the Mother to get rid of Gella, he feels compelled to help her. Eventually, Axel leaves the Path and tries to make amends for his crimes.

> "I'VE SPENT PART OF MY LIFE TRYING TO BE THE PERFECT GREYLARK, AND ANOTHER BEING THE BEST OF THE WORST."
>
> – Axel Greylark

PHAN-TU ZENN

PRONOUNS: He/him
SPECIES: Human
HEIGHT: 1.83 m (6 ft)

ALLEGIANCE: Eiram
FIRST APPEARANCE: Con

Phan-tu Zenn is the adopted son of Queen Adrialla of Eiram. Raised as the heir of Eiram, he takes time out from his royal duties to help people in need. Xiri A'lbaran, the heir of E'ronoh—a planet that has been at war with Eiram for many years—proposes that Phan-tu marries her in order to create a political bond between the two planets. Phan-tu agrees out of a desire for peace. After the initial peace treaty breaks down, the newlyweds remain on their respective planets. But Phan-tu stows away on Xiri's ship when she goes to Dalna to fight against the Path of the Open Hand.

> "WHATEVER WE DO, LET'S DO IT TOGETHER."
> – Phan-tu Zenn to Xiri A'lbaran

XIRI A'LBARAN

PRONOUNS: She/her
SPECIES: Human
HEIGHT: 1.68 m (5 ft 6 in)

ALLEGIANCE: E'ronoh
FIRST APPEARANCE: Con

As the daughter of E'ronoh's monarch, Xiri is raised to rule and fight. She serves as captain of Thylefire Squadron, an elite starfighter unit, and also arranges to marry Phan-tu Zenn, heir of Eiram, hoping to create peace between the two worlds. They fight side by side against the Path of the Open Hand, and a bond develops between them. During the Battle of Dalna, Xiri fights alongside both Eiram and E'ronoh soldiers to defeat the Path's droids. She and Phan-tu go on to create a new peace treaty between Eiram and E'ronoh, ending the war that many feared would go on forever.

> "I AM WILLING TO GIVE EVERYTHING I HAVE, ALL OF ME, TO SECURE THE BEST FUTURE FOR OUR PEOPLE."
> – Xiri A'lbaran

DANK GRAKS GANG LEADER

Vocalizer translates his words into Basic

Hood and cape incorporated into armor

PRONOUNS: He/him
SPECIES: Geonosian
HEIGHT: 1.68 m (5 ft 6 in)

ALLEGIANCE: Dank Graks, Sorcerers of Tund (formerly)
FIRST APPEARANCE: THRA (PII)

Arkik Von was previously affiliated with the Sorcerers of Tund, a mysterious group of dark-side enchanters. Arkik now works to bring together the Dank Graks criminal gang, a collective of outlaws with the same goal as him—wresting control of Takodana away from Maz Kanata and the Jedi.

THE *GRIM DEVOURER*
Arkik travels to Jedha on board his ship, the *Grim Devourer*. He's made a deal with the Path of the Open Hand to help start a war there. He abducts Maz Kanata, and then welcomes Jedi Sav Malagán into the Dank Graks after putting her through some trials. Arkik then returns to Takodana with Maz still his prisoner, and claims the planet as his own.

"MY DEATH-DEALING DROIDS WILL END THEM EXPEDITIOUSLY!"

– Arkik Von

LADY OF ANGCORD

PRONOUNS: She/her
SPECIES: Human
HEIGHT: 1.65 m (5 ft 5 in)

ALLEGIANCE: Angcord
FIRST APPEARANCE: THRA: QotJ

The Lady of Angcord rules a centuries-old kingdom that is the only civilization on the barren planet Angcord. She is protected by her royal guard, the Pilgrim Warriors. The Lady draws power from a Force artifact known as the Echo Stone, but she does not realize it has a dark side. When she notices that something is killing plants and preventing crops from growing, she welcomes help from Jedi Barnabas Vim and Vix Fonnick. Vim reveals the stone's corrupting influence, so the Lady keeps just one piece of it, hoping it can restore life to the planet.

Ceremonial helmet evokes her planet's orbit

Strength and reflexes enhanced by Echo Stone

"I FEAR OUR WORLD IS DYING."

– Lady of Angcord

FIRST PILGRIM

"WOULD YOU LIKE TO SEE WHAT REAL FORCE WARRIORS LOOK LIKE?"

– First Pilgrim

PRONOUNS: He/him
SPECIES: Unknown
HEIGHT: 1.60 m (5 ft 3 in)

ALLEGIANCE: Angcord
FIRST APPEARANCE: THRA: QotJ

The First Pilgrim leads the Lady of Angcord's Pilgrim Warriors, the protectors of the Force-strong Echo Stone. The First Pilgrim is deeply loyal to the Lady, but he doesn't know that the Echo Stone has been corrupting her with its dark-side influence. When Jedi Barnabas Vim and Vix Fonnick arrive to investigate the stone, the First Pilgrim is furious. However, the sight of the Lady's corrupted appearance —a result of the stone's dark-side powers— gives him pause. After the Jedi destroy the stone, the First Pilgrim wants to kill them, but instead he shows his loyalty to the Lady and heeds her command to let them go.

Hooked staff can sweep enemies off their feet

Quilted Pilgrim Guard uniform

BOKANA KOSS

PRONOUNS: He/him
SPECIES: Ovissian
HEIGHT: 1.96 m (6 ft 5 in)

ALLEGIANCE: Path of the Open Hand
FIRST APPEARANCE: PoV

A former mercenary, Bokana Koss is a recent convert to the Path of the Open Hand. Marda Ro and Jedi Silandra Sho rescue him from rioters, and he travels with Marda to Planet X to collect Nameless eggs. Bokana's budding romance with Marda falters after he appears to develop Force abilities. When attacked by monsters on the unfamiliar planet, Bokana pulls one of them away from the ship, sacrificing himself to allow the others to escape.

> "WE'VE ALL BEEN THROUGH THINGS. AND WE ALL HAVE SCARS. WHAT MATTERS IS HOW WE HELP EACH OTHER HEAL."
>
> – Bokana Koss

RAF THATCHBURN

PRONOUNS: He/him
SPECIES: Human
HEIGHT: 1.73 m (5 ft 8 in)

ALLEGIANCE: Galactic Antipiracy Command
FIRST APPEARANCE: THRA (PII)

Inspector Raf Thatchburn is an officer of the law who is out to stop the galaxy's pirates and criminals. However, he hangs out with Maz Kanata's pirate crew after falling in love with one of them, Alak. Raf comes across as quite intense, intimidating people with his grim appearance and Corellian hound, Tanteek. He's quick to fight when he thinks he's under attack, even brawling with his own partner at times. While hunting down the Dank Graks gang, Raf finds himself surrounded until he is rescued by hyperspace prospector Dexter Jettster and Padawan Sav Malagán. He later attempts to arrest Maz's crew, including Alak.

Corellian hound

Breathing mask connected to air filter

"IF YOU'RE HERE TO TRY TO KILL ME, LET'S GET STARTED."

– Raf Thatchburn

VICEROY FERROL

PRONOUNS: He/him
SPECIES: Human
HEIGHT: 1.75 m (5 ft 9 in)
ALLEGIANCE: E'ronoh
FIRST APPEARANCE: Con

Viceroy Ferrol is the advisor to Monarch A'lbaran of E'ronoh. He finds the Jedi and Republic to be bothersome intruders, so he conspires against the peace treaty with Eiram. However, his schemes place him in conflict with the Path of the Open Hand.

"EVEN THE BEST OF US LOSE SIGHT OF WHAT WE'RE FIGHTING FOR."

– Ferrol

REV FERROL

PRONOUNS: He/him
SPECIES: Human
HEIGHT: 1.80 m (5 ft 11 in)
ALLEGIANCE: E'ronoh
FIRST APPEARANCE: Con

Pilot Rev Ferrol agrees with his father, the viceroy, that E'ronoh should destroy Eiram. When serving alongside Xiri A'lbaran in her starfighter squadron, he tries to disrupt Xiri's attempts at peace by kidnapping her and her husband, Phan-tu Zenn, then rams their ship into E'ronoh's capital city. After Xiri escapes, she kills Rev in a starfighter battle.

"I WILL SIT ON THAT THRONE."

– Rev Ferrol

LIAN CEROX

PRONOUNS: She/her
SPECIES: Human
HEIGHT: 1.63 m (5 ft 4 in)
ALLEGIANCE: Eiram
FIRST APPEARANCE: TBoJ

Ambassador Lian Cerox represents Eiram in the peace talks held on Jedha. She believes E'ronoh started the war with her planet, so she doesn't try to stop Eiram soldiers from fighting back. Cerox cuts a deal with former prospector Tilson Graf to make him the mediator of the peace talks, though she is unaware of Tilson's true motives.

"I CANNOT BRING MYSELF TO TRUST THE INTENTIONS OF THE DELEGATES FROM E'RONOH."

– Lian Cerox

TINTAK

PRONOUNS: He/him
SPECIES: Human
HEIGHT: 1.75 m (5 ft 9 in)
ALLEGIANCE: E'ronoh
FIRST APPEARANCE: TBoJ

Tintak is the E'ronoh ambassador at the Eiram–E'ronoh peace talks. He hopes for a peaceful resolution, though he isn't sure one is possible. Despite this, he is charming and energetic, bantering with Jedi Aida Forte. The peace talks are disrupted by riots and, when a speeder crashes into the negotiation rooms, Tintak loses his life.

"YOU NEVER KNOW WHAT TROUBLE'S LURKING..."

– Tintak

QUEEN ADRIALLA

PRONOUNS: She/her
SPECIES: Human
HEIGHT: 1.60 m (5 ft 3 in)

ALLEGIANCE: Eiram
FIRST APPEARANCE: Con

Queen Adrialla rules Eiram with her wife, Odelia. Her people require medical supplies, so she agrees to a ceasefire with rival planet E'ronoh after years of war. However, in a secret deal with the Path of Open Hand, Adrialla manufactures a poison to be used against E'ronoh, though she quickly comes to regret the arrangement. She supports her son, Phan-tu, when he agrees to marry the heir of E'ronoh as part of a peace treaty.

"WE'VE ALL HAD TO MAKE SACRIFICES THESE LAST FEW YEARS."

– Queen Adrialla

MONARCH A'LBARAN

PRONOUNS: He/him
SPECIES: Human
HEIGHT: 1.75 m (5 ft 9 in)

ALLEGIANCE: E'ronoh
FIRST APPEARANCE: Con

Monarch A'lbaran, leader of E'ronoh, has seen his planet embroiled in the bitter Forever War against Eiram for years. The toll of the conflict and the death of his son has led A'lbaran to lose all hope. When his daughter, Xiri, convinces him to agree to a ceasefire, he slowly begins to trust that there may be a pathway to peace.

"I WILL UNLEASH THE FULL MIGHT OF E'RONOH'S FORCES UNTIL THERE IS NOTHING LEFT OF YOUR PLANET BUT SALT."

– Monarch A'lbaran

RIAK

PRONOUNS: He/him
SPECIES: Crulkon
HEIGHT: 1.83 m (6 ft)

ALLEGIANCE: Riak's gang
FIRST APPEARANCE: Yod

Riak is the leader of a Crulkon gang that regularly raids a Scalvi village on the Outer Rim planet Turrak. When Yoda arrives to assist the Scalvi people, Riak is angered by the presence of the Jedi. He tries to force Yoda to help the Crulkon but is killed by a young Scalvi warrior.

MESOOK

PRONOUNS: He/him
SPECIES: Human
HEIGHT: 1.78 m (5 ft 10 in)

ALLEGIANCE: Guardians of the Whills
FIRST APPEARANCE: TBoJ

Mesook is a member of the Guardians of the Whills. He uses a lightbow to help protect the Temple of the Kyber. When his friend Jedi Master Silandra Sho visits Jedha, he gives her a tour of the city. Later, when violence breaks out, he lets the Jedi take the lead in the ensuing battle.

"THE TEMPLE IS A PEACEFUL PLACE, THE GUARDIANS OF THE WHILLS HAVE LITTLE JURISDICTION OUT IN THE WILDS OF THE HOLY CITY."

– Mesook

SAYA KEEM

PRONOUNS: She/her
SPECIES: Zabrak
HEIGHT: 1.88 m (6 ft 2 in)

ALLEGIANCE: Dank Graks
FIRST APPEARANCE:
THRA (PII)

Saya Keem is the teenage pilot of the Dank Graks ship, the *Grim Devourer*. While Keem's fellow gang members are regularly distracted by greed or thoughts of revenge, Keem is more practical and is always considering what her next step should be.

DRRN

PRONOUNS: He/him
SPECIES: Muun
HEIGHT: 1.85 m (6 ft 1 in)

ALLEGIANCE: Dank Graks
FIRST APPEARANCE:
THRA (PII)

Drrn is a member of the Dank Graks criminal gang. He rarely speaks, letting his stern expressions and tall stature leave an impression on outsiders. Drrn hovers in the background most of the time, seemingly everywhere at once, and he lets his fellow Dank Graks members know what he's thinking with grunts and groans.

LAVALOX VERZEN

PRONOUNS: She/her
SPECIES: Cosian
HEIGHT: 1.75 m (5 ft 9 in)

ALLEGIANCE: Dank Graks
FIRST APPEARANCE:
THRA (PII)

Known for speaking mostly in gibberish, Lavalox Verzen operates the guns on the Dank Graks' ship, the *Grim Devourer*. While Verzen delights in firing at enemies, she has exceptionally bad aim. She is also keeping a secret —she's actually Jedi Master Tera Sinube in disguise.

SARETHA VON BEEL

PRONOUNS: She/her
SPECIES: Human
HEIGHT: 1.78 m (5 ft 10 in)

ALLEGIANCE: Unknown
FIRST APPEARANCE: ToE NP

Like most hyperspace prospectors, Saretha von Beel is strong and tough, expecting danger at every turn. She is abducted by pirates while mapping a new path and is later freed by Jedi Knight Lee Harro. After leaving Harro, von Beel lands in the Enlightenment bar on Jedha, where she shares her adventures with the locals.

"SOME PEOPLE NEVER LEARN, ME INCLUDED."

– Saretha von Beel

SICATRA

PRONOUNS: She/her
SPECIES: Human
HEIGHT: 1.80 m (5 ft 11 in)
ALLEGIANCE: Firevale, Bethune
FIRST APPEARANCE: THR: TB

On the planet Gansevor, a fierce rivalry exists between the states of Bethune and Firevale. Princess Sicatra of Bethune joins Prince Colden of Firevale in a plot to overthrow the Firevale queen. However, Sicatra is scheming against Colden as well, though he doesn't know it. Her lies upset both Colden and Jedi Barash Silvain, whom she leaves feeling betrayed.

"WE JUST WANTED OUR CHANCE."

– Sicatra

COLDEN

PRONOUNS: He/him
SPECIES: Human
HEIGHT: 1.83 m (6 ft)
ALLEGIANCE: Firevale
FIRST APPEARANCE: THR: TB

Prince Colden is next in line for the Firevale throne. His rivals in Bethune claim he kidnapped their princess, though that was part of a plot between Colden and Princess Sicatra. Colden deceives his own family, but he is ultimately betrayed by Sicatra's lies.

TOZEN

PRONOUNS: He/him
SPECIES: Human
HEIGHT: 1.78 m (5 ft 10 in)
ALLEGIANCE: Bethune
FIRST APPEARANCE: THR: TB

Field Marshal Tozen leads the Bethune army when it lays siege to Firevale. He believes in Bethune's cause, and despises the mercenaries that fight alongside him since they are only there for the loot they will take after the battle. Tozen is killed by mercenary leader General Viess in a dispute over plunder.

BREE MENAREN

PRONOUNS: He/him
SPECIES: Scalvi
HEIGHT: 1.09 m (3 ft 7 in)
ALLEGIANCE: Scalvi
FIRST APPEARANCE: Yod

Bree Menaren is a Scalvi child who meets Yoda when the Jedi visits his village on Turrak. Yoda tries to get Bree to see both sides of the conflict between the Scalvi and their Crulkon raiders. At first, Bree can't see past the violence they've inflicted. But years later, he finally understands Yoda's lesson and makes peace with the Crulkon.

TY YORRICK

Ty is no longer a Jedi but keeps her lightsaber

Many Tholothians wear headdresses around their head tendrils

Lightsaber holster

PRONOUNS: She/her
SPECIES: Tholothian
HEIGHT: 1.70 m (5 ft 7 in)

ALLEGIANCE: Jedi Order (formerly)
FIRST APPEARANCE: TRS

Ty Yorrick, once known as Tylera, left the Jedi Order after she felt forced to kill a fellow Padawan who had been overcome by the dark side. Ty now works as a saber-for-hire who specializes in hunting dangerous monsters across the galaxy. She likes to work alone, but is aided by two droids, KL-03, a sarcastic protocol droid, and an astromech named RO-VR.

BACK AMONG JEDI

Yorrick takes a job as a bodyguard for inventor Mantessa Chekkat at the Republic Fair on Valo, despite her concerns about being around a large number of Jedi. But during the chaos of the Nihil attack, Yorrick and Jedi Master Elzar Mann connect to each other through the Force and work to calm dangerous predators that have escaped the Valo zoo. Yorrick later joins forces with the Jedi again during the Battle of Grizal.

> "THE FORCE IS IN ALL THINGS. THAT'S WHAT MY MASTER USED TO SAY."
>
> – Ty Yorrick

ZEEN MRALA

FORCE-SENSITIVE MIKKIAN

Head tendrils

Layered tunic

PRONOUNS: She/her
SPECIES: Mikkian
HEIGHT: 1.65 m (5 ft 5 in)

ALLEGIANCE: Elders of the Path, Jedi Order
FIRST APPEARANCE: THRA (PI)

Separated from her parents as a child, Zeen Mrala grows up on the planet Trymant IV, hiding her Force abilities—even from her best friend, Krix Kamerat. She is a member of the Elders of the Path, a group that believes using the Force is wrong. When Zeen finally uses her abilities, she finds freedom but loses her connection to Krix, who feels betrayed.

NEW FRIENDS
When fallout from the Great Disaster threatens her planet, Trymant IV, Zeen uses the Force to help minimize damage. A group of Jedi, including Lula Talisola and Yoda, assist Zeen and offer her shelter on Starlight Beacon soon after. While Zeen is deemed too old to train as a Jedi, she is welcomed on board and receives instructions on how to better control the abilities she has.

"THEY'RE LIKE ME! I... I COULD BE LIKE THEM!"
— Zeen Mrala

AVON STARROS

PRECOCIOUS INVENTOR

Scouting goggles

Wrist guard Avon made herself

PRONOUNS: She/her
SPECIES: Human
HEIGHT: 1.52 m (5 ft)

ALLEGIANCE: Starros clan
FIRST APPEARANCE: AToC

Avon Starros is a brilliant young inventor. Quick to break rules that slow her down when solving problems, Avon both frustrates and impresses those around her. Some of her inventions include antigravity inserts and simulated kyber crystals. When faced with a dangerous situation, Avon is bold and decisive in her actions, which serves her well when she is captured by the Nihil. Avon believes technology can solve any problem, so she is initially skeptical of the Jedi.

SELF-PROGRAMMED DROID

J-6 is Avon's protocol droid, reprogrammed from a nanny droid to a companion droid with useful protection and surveillance skills. Avon installs new software into J-6 that allows the droid to gradually reprogram herself, leading J-6 to exhibit a unique personality and attitude.

"OK, KEEP YOUR SECRETS, JEDI."

– Avon Starros to Vernestra Rwoh

SIAN HOLT

PRIVATE INVESTIGATOR

Jacket made from elite chaughaine fabric

PRONOUNS: She/her
SPECIES: Human
HEIGHT: 1.65 m (5 ft 5 in)

ALLEGIANCE: Her clients
FIRST APPEARANCE: THR: ToS

Sian Holt is a tough, no-nonsense private investigator. Hired by Chancellor Lina Soh, Sian works with Jedi Master Emerick Caphtor to discover who or what killed Jedi Loden Greatstorm. Holt has a sharp sense of humor, loves music, and is willing to bend the truth to get her way, but when she takes on a job, nothing will stop her from closing the case.

TAKING CHARGE

Following a lead on the case, Emerick starts hallucinating after being exposed to the Nameless on a freighter. Meanwhile, criminal Arathab Fal threatens another passenger, the spy Beesar Tal-Apurna. Taking control of the situation, Sian grabs Emerick's lightsaber, attacks Arathab, and moves Emerick away before the Nameless can do more damage.

> "REVENGE IS EXPENSIVE, BORING, AND NOT NEARLY AS SATISFYING AS THE HOLOS MAKE IT OUT TO BE."
> – Sian Holt

MYARGA ANJILIAC ATIRUE

HUTT WARLORD

Skulls of enemies defeated during her rise to power

Muscular tail helps her move at high speed

Armored Kamril MK-X hoversled

PRONOUNS: She/her
SPECIES: Hutt
HEIGHT: 1.57 m (5 ft 2 in)

ALLEGIANCE: Hutt clan
FIRST APPEARANCE: THR (PI)

Myarga the Hutt is known for being both generous and merciless. Her attitudes shift as the situations change, but one thing is always true—she's out for herself. She commands an army of starships and rancor riders, and her hoversled keeps her safe, floating above the battlefield. Myarga becomes a reluctant ally to the Jedi in their fight against the Drengir on the planet Sedri Minor. She realizes she needs all the help she can get to defeat the Drengir.

CAPTURED BY THE NIHIL

When the Jedi track down the Drengir known as the Great Progenitor, Myarga wants to destroy her. Jedi Avar Kriss convinces her not to, but their shared mission fails to create a bond between the Hutt and the Jedi. Instead, when Myarga next meets a Jedi—Keeve Trennis—the Hutt exposes her to the Nihil.

"TEAR THEM LIMB FROM LIMB!"

– Myarga

AFFIE HOLLOW

CAPTAIN OF THE *VESSEL*

Flight suit includes emergency seals to close rips or tears

Blaster saw use during the Amaxine station incident

PRONOUNS: She/her
SPECIES: Human
HEIGHT: 1.68 m (5 ft 6 in)

ALLEGIANCE: The *Vessel*, Byne Guild (formerly)
FIRST APPEARANCE: ItD

Affie Hollow started out as an apprentice on the transport ship *Vessel*, working with pilot Leox Gyasi and navigator Geode. Her assertive and practical nature helps her make good decisions, and Affie is now the owner and loyal captain of the ship. Her time on the *Vessel* has made her a skilled and well-traveled spacer.

EXPOSING THE BYNE GUILD

As an apprentice, Affie works for the Byne Guild, transporting legal and outlawed cargo across the galaxy. She later discovers that her foster mother, Guild leader Scover Byne, was responsible for the deaths of her birth parents. Despite her love for Scover, Affie makes a brave choice and reports the Guild's abusive tactics to the Republic.

"WHAT KIND OF CAPTAIN ABANDONS HER PEOPLE?"

– Affie Hollow

LEOX GYASI

PRONOUNS: He/him
SPECIES: Human
HEIGHT: 1.80 m (5 ft 11 in)

ALLEGIANCE: Galactic Republic, Byne Guild (formerly)
FIRST APPEARANCE: ItD

Pilot Leox Gyasi usually appears calm and collected, even during times of stress. His happy-go-lucky, spiritual attitude means he doesn't tend to worry about his not-quite-legal cargo. Despite his smuggling activities, Leox has a heart of gold, a desire to help all sentient beings, and a feeling of goodwill toward the Republic.

Comlink set into fashionable vest

Boots with hidden pockets

"UNDER THE SCANNERS IS OUR EXPERTISE!"
– Leox Gyasi

GEODE

PRONOUNS: He/him
SPECIES: Vintian
HEIGHT: 1.73 m (5 ft 8 in)

ALLEGIANCE: Galactic Republic, Byne Guild (formerly)
FIRST APPEARANCE: ItD

Although Geode resembles a large rock, and never visibly speaks or moves, he is somehow often in the right place at the right time. During the Great Disaster, he navigates the *Vessel* through a chaotic region of hyperspace with his crewmates, Leox Gyasi and Affie Hollow. He also saves Padawan Reath Silas' life by knocking him away from an open airlock.

Rocklike surface lightly sparkles in hyperspace

"GOOD PICK, GEODE!"
– Affie Hollow to Geode

SYLVESTRI YARROW

SWITCHBACK PILOT

Rifle secured in backpack holster

Flight gear pants

PRONOUNS: She/her
SPECIES: Human
HEIGHT: 1.57 m (5 ft 2 in)

ALLEGIANCE: Byne Guild
FIRST APPEARANCE: OotS

Sylvestri Yarrow is the pilot of the *Switchback*, a cargo ship she inherited from her mother, Chancey. As far as Sylvestri knows, Chancey was killed by the Nihil. Along with her copilot, Neeto Janajana, Sylvestri does her best to keep her shipping business afloat. She is more comfortable fixing things or evading pirates than making small talk with politicians or high society. But after her ship is forced out of hyperspace, Sylvestri crosses paths with the wealthy physicist Xylan Graf, who shakes up what she knows to be true about her past.

ROUGH LESSONS

Sylvestri's mother secretly worked for the Nihil, so Sylvestri spent part of her youth being trained by a female Twi'lek she called "Auntie Lourna." Auntie Lourna was actually Nihil Tempest Runner Lourna Dee, and her brutal self-defense and combat lessons often left Sylvestri injured.

M-227

M-227 is Sylvestri's ancient security droid. More than 200 years old, M-227 used to belong to Sylvestri's mother.

> "A CAPTAIN DOESN'T QUIT THEIR SHIP, NO MATTER HOW BLEAK THINGS GET."
>
> – Sylvestri Yarrow

JORDANNA SPARKBURN

SAN TEKKA CLAN DEPUTY

Vollka horns conduct electricity

Utility belt carries a variety of weapons

PRONOUNS: She/her
SPECIES: Human
HEIGHT: 1.73 m (5 ft 8 in)

ALLEGIANCE: San Tekka clan
FIRST APPEARANCE: OotS

Jordanna Sparkburn is deputy of the San Tekka clan on the desert planet Tiikae. Years of protecting the locals from threats including the Nihil, Zygerrians, Drengir, and Hutts have left Jordanna hardened to the world. She is blunt with her words and quick to turn to violence. However, she finds a soft spot for pilot Sylvestri Yarrow, and the two develop romantic feelings for each other during the brief time Sylvestri stays on Tiikae.

NIHIL KNOWLEDGE

Jordanna's experience with the Nihil becomes a battle advantage once she leaves Tiikae. Her previous exposure to Nihil knockout gas helps her recover quickly when she and two Jedi are ambushed. Later, Jordanna puts together a deadly Nihil weapon she's kept from her Tiikae days to use while rescuing Sylvestri.

VOLLKA COMPANION

Jordanna travels with a vollka she names Remy. Vollka are such fast creatures that some believe they can achieve invisibility while chasing their prey.

> ## "IN THE PAST YEAR THIS PLANET HAS BECOME A WAR ZONE."
>
> – Jordanna Sparkburn

Long, sharp talons make Remy a fierce hunter

ALYS "CRASH" ONGWA

PRONOUNS: She/her
SPECIES: Human
HEIGHT: 1.78 m (5 ft 10 in)

ALLEGIANCE: Crash's crew
FIRST APPEARANCE: THRA: A

Alys Ongwa, nicknamed "Crash," has run the Supreme Coronet City Diplomat Protection business since she was a teenager, offering bodyguard services to politicians on Corellia. She is hired to protect Republic Chancellor Lina Soh when she visits, and later joins forces with the Jedi when the Nihil infiltrate the Coronet City police. Crash is reckless, trusts no one, and has a chaotic style, but she is respected for always getting the job done. She speaks several languages, which allows her to listen in on conversations others assume she can't understand.

CRASH'S CREW

SPECIES: Assorted
HEIGHT: Various

ALLEGIANCE: Crash's crew, Alys "Crash" Ongwa
FIRST APPEARANCE: THRA: A

The crew employed by Alys "Crash" Ongwa for her protection business on Corellia can be counted on to get the job done. Crew members come from all over the galaxy, and include Dowutin pilot Fezzonk, the Ovarto Bitolo-Bash, the Weequay Barchibar, an Arcona named Smeemarm, a Wookiee named Tangor, and Crash's best friend, the Grindalid Prybolt Garavult. The crew is assisted by 10-K8, Crash's sassy security droid, who is known to sing to herself while gathering information. When Prybolt and Ovarto are killed guarding a Coronet City dignitary, Crash and her crew work together to find the culprits.

"ALL GOOD IN THE UNDERBELLY."
– Smeemarm

RHIL DAIRO

PRONOUNS: She/her
SPECIES: Human
HEIGHT: 1.65 m (5 ft 5 in)

ALLEGIANCE: GoNet
FIRST APPEARANCE: TRS

GoNet journalist Rhil Dairo cares deeply about reporting the news and the people affected by her stories. Her camera droid, T-9, records everything so Dairo's reporting can focus on facts, not fluff. A cybernetic implant over one eye connects to her droid, allowing Dairo to communicate silently with T-9 when necessary. She travels with Chancellor Lina Soh and Jedi Master Stellan Gios to Valo to cover the Republic Fair. After the Nihil strike on the Fair, Dairo uses her communications and tech skills to send a distress signal from the planet.

Microphone

GoNet ID badge

"I WANT PEOPLE TO SEE THIS. I WANT THEM TO KNOW WHAT IT'S LIKE."

– Rhil Dairo

VANE SARPO

PRONOUNS: He/him
SPECIES: Vuman
HEIGHT: 1.78 m (5 ft 10 in)

ALLEGIANCE: None
FIRST APPEARANCE: SS: PM

A self-described soldier of fortune, Vane Sarpo reunites with his old flame, Velko Jahen, when he arrives at Starlight Beacon. Sarpo tells Velko—now an administrative aide on Starlight—that he is a trader selling figurines. Sarpo is just as charming as Jahen remembers from their brief relationship during the Soikan Civil War, but that doesn't stop Jahen from jailing him upon discovering Nihil weapons under his stash of souvenirs. But things are not as they seem: it is soon revealed that Sarpo is an unwilling victim of the Nihil, who have been controlling him via a tattoo rigged to detonate if he doesn't follow their plan.

KEEFAR BRANTO

PRONOUNS: He/him
SPECIES: Human
HEIGHT: 1.70 m (5 ft 7 in)

ALLEGIANCE: None
FIRST APPEARANCE: THR: ToS

Keefar Branto is a career criminal with a past that includes bounty hunting, gunrunning, and a stint with the Nihil, before private investigator Sian Holt agrees to partner up with him. During an undercover operation for the Republic so secret even Holt doesn't know about it, Branto is murdered by the criminal Arathab Fal.

KLERIN CHEKKAT

PRONOUNS: She/her
SPECIES: Kuranu
HEIGHT: 1.65 m (5 ft 5 in)

ALLEGIANCE: None
FIRST APPEARANCE: TRS

Klerin Chekkat is an inventor who travels with her mother, Mantessa, and their hired bodyguard, Ty Yorrick, to the Republic Fair on Valo. Mantessa tries to sell a prototype of a nullifier device—which can disable blasters and lightsabers—to a senator. But the deal is unsuccessful, so Klerin tries to strike her own deal with the Nihil.

> "MY MOTHER TOOK CREDIT FOR THE DEVICE, BUT IT WAS MY WORK."
>
> – Klerin Chekkat

THADDEUS WOLK

PRONOUNS: He/him
SPECIES: Gungan
HEIGHT: 1.96 m (6 ft 5 in)

ALLEGIANCE: Unknown
FIRST APPEARANCE: OotS

Thaddeus Wolk is a Gungan scientist who specializes in theoretical hyperspace physics. While a professor at the Academy of Carida, he taught Chancey Yarrow. Later, Wolk suspects Chancey's involvement in the Nihil attacks that somehow pull ships out of hyperspace, because he remembers her obsession with building a gravity well.

> "MS. YARROW, YOUR MOTHER IS ALIVE, AND SHE IS WORKING WITH THE NIHIL."
>
> – Thaddeus Wolk to Sylvestri Yarrow

NEETO JANAJANA

PRONOUNS: He/him
SPECIES: Sullustan
HEIGHT: 1.73 m (5 ft 8 in)
ALLEGIANCE: Sylvestri Yarrow

FIRST APPEARANCE: OotS

Neeto Janajana is the level-headed copilot of the *Switchback*, owned by cargo trader Sylvestri Yarrow. Janajana used to work for Sylvestri's mother, Chancey, before she was presumed dead. When the *Switchback* is pulled out of hyperspace and captured by the Nihil, Janajana helps convince Sylvestri that her life is more important than her ship.

MARI SAN TEKKA

HYPERSPACE PATH CREATOR

Medical equipment prolongs Mari's life

Electro-shocks help control Mari

PRONOUNS: She/her
SPECIES: Human
HEIGHT: 1.68 m (5 ft 6 in)

ALLEGIANCE: San Tekka clan
FIRST APPEARANCE: LotJ

Mari San Tekka is part of the San Tekka clan, wealthy hyperspace prospectors who map and sell safe passageways through hyperspace. As a child, Mari exhibits a unique ability to find paths that others cannot see. She is soon abducted by the Ro family, who use her special gifts to gain an advantage in their Nihil raids. The Nihil place Mari in a medical capsule that keeps her alive but imprisoned for more than a century on Marchion Ro's ship, the *Gaze Electric*.

REACHING OUT

Mari is frail but she still enjoys charting new hyperspace routes, even though she does not realize who she is now creating them for. Mari speaks telepathically with Jedi Master Loden Greatstorm when he is held captive on the *Gaze Electric*. Their conversations bring Mari a sense of peace and help Loden focus his powers for long enough to break free.

> "I HAVE A GIFT FOR YOU. ONE LAST PATH BEFORE I PASS ON. IT WAS ALWAYS MEANT FOR YOU."
>
> – Mari San Tekka

XYLAN GRAF

Cape made from Cantonican gold silk

Graf family heirloom

PRONOUNS: He/him
SPECIES: Human
HEIGHT: 1.75 m (5 ft 9 in)

ALLEGIANCE: Graf family
FIRST APPEARANCE: OotS

Everything about physicist Xylan Graf screams wealth, from his expensive clothing to the way he assumes that people around him will do what he wants without asking any questions. A member of the powerful Graf family —who made their fortune mapping hyperspace lanes—Xylan approaches pilot Sylvestri Yarrow with a proposal to help solve a hyperspace mystery. But Xylan doesn't tell Sylvestri the whole truth, instead concealing his true objective, which is to take ownership of as many hyperspace lanes as he can.

"IT IS EXACTLY WHAT MY FAMILY NEEDS: A VAST, UNOCCUPIED AREA OF SPACE."

– Xylan Graf

SHUG DRABOR

Falumpaset cheese

PRONOUNS: He/him
SPECIES: Anzellan
HEIGHT: 23 cm (9 in)

ALLEGIANCE: Chandrila Charter Company
FIRST APPEARANCE: MH

Shug Drabor is an Anzellan engineer stationed in Coronet City on the planet Corellia. Drabor is the founder of the Chandrila Charter Company and the designer of its luxury ships. He oversees the construction of MPO-1400 *Purrgil*-class starcruisers, which include the *Halcyon*, the company's most well-known ship. Drabor's knowledge of ships is vast and he is always intensely proud of his work. When the engineering enthusiast Padawan Ram Jomaram spends time on Corellia, Drabor befriends the young Jedi. He also encourages the crew of the *Halcyon* to fight back against the Nihil during an attack.

"TIME TO FIGHT FOR THE *HALCYON*!"

– Shug Drabor

MARLOWE SAN TEKKA

PRONOUNS: He/him
SPECIES: Human
HEIGHT: 1.70 m (5 ft 7 in)
ALLEGIANCE: San Tekka clan

FIRST APPEARANCE: LotJ

Marlowe San Tekka and his husband, Vellis, are wealthy hyperspace prospectors who made their fortune selling travel routes to traders, governments, and entrepreneurs. After the Great Disaster, Jedi Elzar Mann and Avar Kriss visit Marlowe, asking him to help with Keven Tarr's droid network that will predict falling debris.

VELLIS SAN TEKKA

PRONOUNS: He/him
SPECIES: Human
HEIGHT: 1.75 m (5 ft 9 in)
ALLEGIANCE: San Tekka clan
FIRST APPEARANCE: LotJ

When hyperspace expert Vellis San Tekka and his husband, Marlowe, hear the details of the Great Disaster they are perplexed, since hyperspace paths are designed to be empty. After asking if mutiny or a ship malfunction might have been the cause, Vellis wonders if a San Tekka long thought lost could be involved.

CATRIONA GRAF

PRONOUNS: She/her
SPECIES: Human
HEIGHT: 1.60 m (5 ft 3 in)
ALLEGIANCE: Graf family
FIRST APPEARANCE: OotS

Catriona Graf is the head of the powerful Graf family, who made their money selling hyperspace paths. She is one of the main sources of funding for the space station Starlight Beacon, but Catriona keeps her business dealings as secret as possible. She works with the Nihil and also funds Lourna Dee's gravity-well projector with Chancey Yarrow.

CHAM CHAM

PRONOUNS: He/him
SPECIES: Cru
HEIGHT: 36 cm (1 ft 2 in)
ALLEGIANCE: Zeen Mrala

FIRST APPEARANCE: THRA (PI)

Cham Cham is Zeen Mrala's pet and loyal friend. Cham Cham can fly but is more often found sitting on Zeen's shoulder. He is with Zeen when the Nihil attack her homeworld, Trymant IV. Master Yoda takes Cham Cham with him when he tries to convince Zeen's friend Krix Kamerat to leave the Nihil.

HACKRACK BEP

PRONOUNS: He/him
SPECIES: Theelin
HEIGHT: 1.73 m (5 ft 8 in)

ALLEGIANCE: Dalna
FIRST APPEARANCE: SS: SR

At first, Vice President Hackrack Bep of Dalna rejects Jedi Vernestra Rwoh's concern that the Nihil pose any threat to Dalna. But Bep is hiding something from the Jedi. In fact, the Nihil have kidnapped Bep's son, Theo, and are threatening to set off explosions along one of the planet's fault lines, which will start a chain reaction of destruction.

"TWO JEDI CANNOT PROTECT AN ENTIRE PLANET."

– Hackrack Bep

ATTICHITCUK

PRONOUNS: He/him
SPECIES: Wookiee
HEIGHT: 2.26 m (7 ft 5 in)

ALLEGIANCE: Wookiee clan
FIRST APPEARANCE: LD

The Wookiee Attichitcuk calls Jedi Knight Nib Assek and her Padawan, Burryaga, to Kashyyyk when the ancient Tree of Life begins to wilt. Nib discovers that the ornaments decorating the Tree of Life are in fact Drengir vines, so Attichitcuk and other local Wookiees help destroy them. Years later, Attichitcuk has a son, whom he names Chewbacca.

HONESTY WEFT

PRONOUNS: He/him
SPECIES: Human
HEIGHT: 1.68 m (5 ft 6 in)

ALLEGIANCE: Dalna
FIRST APPEARANCE: AToC

Honesty Weft feels trapped in his role as the son of a Dalnan ambassador, but he goes with his father on a trip to Starlight Beacon. His father hopes the trip will give Honesty a wider

perspective on the galaxy. While Honesty usually embraces rules, he seeks revenge against the Nihil when they kill his father.

KOLEY LINN

PRONOUNS: He/him
SPECIES: Human
HEIGHT: 1.78 m (5 ft 10 in)

ALLEGIANCE: Byne Guild
FIRST APPEARANCE: TFS

Ace of Staves pilot Koley Linn has a sour temperament and is known for seeking revenge against those he feels have wronged him. While docked at Starlight Beacon, Linn sets out to rob neighboring ships. After a Nihil bomb explodes, Linn's behavior worsens as he tries to escape from Starlight. He is killed by his own rebounding blaster fire after taking a child hostage to try to force his way out.

"I CAN HELP OUT. FOR A PRICE."

– Koley Linn

BEESAR TAL-APURNA

PRONOUNS: She/her
SPECIES: Chadra-Fan
HEIGHT: 1 m (3 ft 3 in)

ALLEGIANCE: Galactic Republic
FIRST APPEARANCE: THR: ToS

Beesar Tal-Apurna grieves over the death of her partner, the Republic pilot Teemank, who was killed during a battle with the Nihil. So when Jedi Emerick Caphtor calls for a spy to follow Nihil doctor Kisma Uttersond, Beesar answers. She stows away on Uttersond's ship and keeps an eye on him, even when the journey proves perilous.

BARTOL

PRONOUNS: He/him
SPECIES: Human
HEIGHT: 1.37 m (4 ft 6 in)

ALLEGIANCE: Sedri Minor community
FIRST APPEARANCE: THRA (PI)

Bartol is an adventurous boy from a farming colony on the planet Sedri Minor. He invites himself along when Jedi Keeve Trennis investigates a Drengir infestation. Keeve and Jedi Master Avar Kriss return Bartol safely to the colony—but only after all three are nearly made part of the Drengir's root-mind.

GLENNA KIP

PRONOUNS: She/her
SPECIES: Shani
HEIGHT: 1.65 m (5 ft 5 in)

ALLEGIANCE: Galactic Republic
FIRST APPEARANCE: MtD

A well-known Republic scientist, Professor Glenna Kip works out of a small lab at Port Haileap. She mentors aspiring young inventor Avon Starros in her pursuit of knowledge. Glenna teaches Avon about synthesizing kyber crystals, a skill that later comes in handy when Avon is kidnapped by the Nihil to build weapons.

"PREPARE YOUR SAMPLES."

– Glenna Kip

KALO SULMAN

PRONOUNS: He/him
SPECIES: Artiodac
HEIGHT: 1.98 m (6 ft 6 in)

ALLEGIANCE: Sedri Minor community, Hutt clan
FIRST APPEARANCE: THRA (PI)

As the speaker of his Sedri Minor colony, Kalo Sulman is the leader—and he rules through threats of violence. He resents Jedi Masters Sskeer and Avar Kriss when they arrive to investigate his colony's crops. In fact, he goes so far as to make a deal with the Hutts instead.

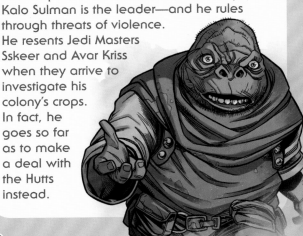

ARATHAB FAL

PRONOUNS: He/him
SPECIES: Tarnab
HEIGHT: 2 m (6 ft 7 in)
ALLEGIANCE: Himself
FIRST APPEARANCE: THR: ToS

Arathab Fal is wanted for murder—though he has other things on his mind. He has a mysterious weapon that could defeat the Jedi. The Nihil want to take it by force, and Fal fights both them and the Jedi to keep possession of it. Detective Sian Holt cuts off Fal's arm with Jedi Emerick Caphtor's lightsaber.

XIMPI

SPECIES: Ximpi
HEIGHT: 28 cm (11 in)
ALLEGIANCE: Ximpi
FIRST APPEARANCE: THR (PI)

The Ximpi are a small, flying species native to the planet Shuraden. Jedi Keeve Trennis encounters two Ximpi, Kanrii and Lekaki, during her Jedi Trials. Originally tasked with retrieving an item from the top of a high spire, Keeve passes her Trials when she diverts from the mission to save a Ximpi city from a swarm of giant insects.

DREWEN

PRONOUNS: He/him
SPECIES: Segredo
HEIGHT: 1.57 m (5 ft 2 in)
ALLEGIANCE: Loreth colony
FIRST APPEARANCE: THRA: TMoTP

At a busy spaceport, curious traveler Drewen overhears that a monster hunter is on a mission to capture a gundark. He follows the monster hunter, Ty Yorrick, into the wilds of the Loreth colony but discovers that the colony's leaders are setting Ty up to fail.

RUU

PRONOUNS: He/him
SPECIES: Lucem
HEIGHT: 1.70 m (5 ft 7 in)
ALLEGIANCE: Jedi Order (formerly)
FIRST APPEARANCE: ToLaL

Previously a shy, thoughtful Padawan, Ruu loses all faith in the Jedi Order after his master, Conithr, is killed by the Nihil—a tragedy he thinks could have been avoided if other Jedi had been around to back her up. Seeking justice above all else, Ruu abandons his Padawan life. Clad in black, wearing a Nihil mask that only just reveals his glittering black eyes, and wielding a lightsaber and blaster, Ruu hunts down the Nihil on the war-torn streets of Coronet City.

BREEBAK & TIP

PRONOUNS: Both: He/him
SPECIES: Bonbrak
HEIGHT: 33 cm (1 ft 1 in)
ALLEGIANCE: Galactic Republic
FIRST APPEARANCE: RtCT

Breebak and goggles-wearing Tip are two of the many Bonbraks who work alongside Jedi mechanic Ram Jomaram in his garage. They help Ram fix a broken communications tower on Valo, swapping out parts from Ram's droid, V-18, to help repair the comms system.

LORD ISAMER

PRONOUNS: He/him
SPECIES: Lasat
HEIGHT: 2.16 m (7 ft 1 in)
ALLEGIANCE: Directorate
FIRST APPEARANCE: ItD

Lord Isamer, a boss in the Directorate criminal gang, is hired by the Hutts to capture the rulers of the planets Eiram and E'ronoh. Isamer wants riches, and is willing to enslave and murder others to feed his greed. He kills Monarch Cassel of E'ronoh, but later falls to Jedi Master Laret Soveral's lightsaber.

"IF ANYONE SURVIVED, MAKE SURE THEY DON'T SURVIVE MUCH LONGER."

– Lord Isamer

SVI'NO ATCHAPAT

PRONOUNS: She/her
SPECIES: Taymar
HEIGHT: 1.68 m (5 ft 6 in)
ALLEGIANCE: Supreme Coronet City Diplomat Protection, Galactic Republic
FIRST APPEARANCE: MH

Svi'no Atchapat is famous throughout the galaxy for her singing. She also performs in scenarios her friend Alys "Crash" Ongwa cooks up to promote Crash's bodyguard business, Supreme Coronet City Diplomat Protection. When the Nihil try to take over the Coronet City shipyards, Svi'no helps the Jedi uncover the plot and stop it.

"IT FEELS GOOD TO LET PEOPLE IN SOMETIMES, HUH?"

– Svi'no Atchapat to Alys Ongwa

BANCHIIANS

SPECIES: Banchiian
HEIGHT: 26 cm (10 in)
ALLEGIANCE: Banchii
FIRST APPEARANCE: TEoB, V1

Native Banchiians lived on their planet, Banchii, long before Republic explorers founded an outpost there. Tiny in size, they hide away from newcomers until they meet the Jedi Lily Tora-Asi, who helps them negotiate for fair trade with the Republic outpost.

INDEX

Senior Editor Matt Jones
Project Art Editor Chris Gould
Production Editor Marc Staples
Senior Production Controller Mary Slater
Managing Editor Emma Grange
Managing Art Editor Vicky Short
Publishing Director Mark Searle

Edited for DK by Shari Last
Designed for DK by Callum Midson,
Ian Midson, and Sandra Perry

For Lucasfilm
Senior Editor Brett Rector
Editor Jennifer Pooley
Creative Director Michael Siglain
Art Director Troy Alders
Story Group Leland Chee, Pablo Hidalgo,
Kate Izquierdo, Matt Martin, Kelsey Sharpe,
Emily Shkoukani, Phil Szostak
Asset Management Chris Argyropoulos,
Gabrielle Levenson, Micaela McCauley,
Elinor De La Torre, Michael Trobiani,
Sarah Williams

DK would like to thank: Megan Crouse and Amy Richau;
Megan Douglass for providing an initial proofread and
Americanization; Julia March for proofreading;
Vanessa Bird for the index; Alexander Evangeli for
picture research; Chelsea Alon at Disney;
Lindsay Burke and Robert Simpson at Lucasfilm;
and *The High Republic* authors, Zoraida Córdova,
Tessa Gratton, Claudia Gray, Justina Ireland,
Lydia Kang, George Mann, Daniel José Older,
Cavan Scott, Charles Soule, and Alyssa Wong.

First American Edition, 2023
Published in the United States by DK Publishing
1745 Broadway, 20th Floor, New York, NY 10019

© & TM 2023 LUCASFILM LTD.

Page design copyright © 2023 Dorling Kindersley Limited
DK, a Division of Penguin Random House LLC
24 25 26 27 10 9 8 7 6 5 4 3 2

003-334314-December/2023

All rights reserved.
Without limiting the rights under the copyright reserved above,
no part of this publication may be reproduced, stored in or
introduced into a retrieval system, or transmitted, in any form,
or by any means (electronic, mechanical, photocopying,
recording, or otherwise), without the prior written
permission of the copyright owner.

Published in Great Britain by Dorling Kindersley Limited

A catalog record for this book is available
from the Library of Congress.

ISBN: 978-0-7440-8468-9

DK books are available at special discounts when purchased in
bulk for sales promotions, premiums, fundraising, or educational
use. For details, contact: DK Publishing Special Markets,
1745 Broadway, 20th Floor, New York, NY 10019
SpecialSales@dk.com

Printed and bound in China

www.dk.com

www.starwars.com

MIX
Paper | Supporting
responsible forestry
FSC™ C018179

This book was made with Forest
Stewardship Council™ certified
paper—one small step in DK's
commitment to a sustainable future.
For more information go to
www.dk.com/our-green-pledge